The
Eye in the Mandala

PATRICK WHITE: A VISION OF
MAN AND GOD

The
Eye in the Mandala

PATRICK WHITE: A VISION OF MAN AND GOD

Peter Beatson

BARNES & NOBLE

BOOKS

10 East 53d St., New York 10022
(a division of Harper & Row Publishers, Inc.)

Published in the U.S.A. 1976 by
HARPER & ROW PUBLISHERS, INC.
BARNES & NOBLE IMPORT DIVISION

First published 1976 by Elek Books Limited, London

Copyright © 1976 Peter Beatson

ISBN 0–06–490331–1

Printed in Great Britain

For
Marjorie and Pat Beatson

Contents

Acknowledgements

I would like to thank Professor Muriel Bradbrook, of Girton College, Cambridge, for her support and encouragement of my work at a time when Patrick White was not as academically orthodox as he is today. I am indebted to Dr Clem Semmler of the Australian Broadcasting Commission, who went out of his way on several occasions to help me with material and who was very kind to me during my visits to Sydney. Mrs Peggy Garland, of Eynsham, Oxfordshire, was a source of encouragement through her enthusiasm for discussing with me her cousin's writing. I would like to thank John Chesshyre for his interest in this book and his extremely helpful suggestions concerning details of wording and structure. Above all I would like to thank Mr White himself for the hospitality he has extended to me in Sydney and for his willingness to indicate to me the works of religious philosophy that he has found congenial.

I would also like to thank those who have spent long and boring hours helping me with the practical side of this book. Of the long list of people to whom I am indebted, and to all of whom I am grateful, I would particularly like to mention my father and Miss Rana Helmi on whose shoulders the main weight of the final drafts fell.

I am grateful to the following for permission to quote copyright material: Patrick White, Curtis Brown Ltd, and The Viking Press Inc. for the extracts from Patrick White's works; Collins Publishers for quotations from Gabriel Marcel, *Being and Having* (translated by A. and C. Black); Routledge & Kegan Paul Ltd and Princeton University Press for quotations from *The Collected Works of C. G. Jung* (edited by Gerhard Adler, Michael Fordham, William McGuire and Herbert Read; translated by R. F. C. Hull), Bollingen Series XX, vol. 12, *Psychology and Alchemy* (copyright 1953 and © 1968 by Bollingen Foundation); T. & T. Clark Limited for the quotation from Martin Buber, *I and Thou* (translated by Ronald Gregor Smith); Routledge & Kegan Paul Ltd and

Note on abbreviations and editions of Patrick White's works

The following abbreviations have been used throughout when quoting from Patrick White's works. Page references in the text are to the edition indicated with an asterisk. For the convenience of the reader details of any later British hardback editions have been included, together with details of first and subsequent US hardback editions, and the latest British and US paperback editions. Further titles are to be reprinted in Jonathan Cape's Uniform Editions in future years.

HV *Happy Valley* London, Harrap, 1939;* New York, Viking, 1940

LD *The Living and the Dead* London, Routledge & Kegan Paul, 1941; Eyre and Spottiswoode, 1962;* Harmondsworth, Penguin, 1975; New York, Viking, 1941

AS *The Aunt's Story* London, Routledge & Kegan Paul, 1948; Eyre and Spottiswoode, 1958;* Harmondsworth, Penguin, 1976; New York, Viking, 1948 and 1974; Avon Books, 1975

TM *The Tree of Man* London, Eyre and Spottiswoode, 1956;* Jonathan Cape, 1974; Harmondsworth, Penguin, 1975; New York, Viking, 1955 and 1974; Avon Books, 1975

V *Voss* London, Eyre and Spottiswoode, 1957;* Harmondsworth, Penguin, 1975; New York, Viking, 1957 and 1974; Avon Books, 1975

RC *Riders in the Chariot* London, Eyre and Spottiswoode, 1961;* Jonathan Cape, Uniform Edition, 1976; Harmondsworth, Penguin, 1976; New York, Viking, 1961 and 1974; Avon Books, 1975

BO *The Burnt Ones* London, Eyre and Spottiswoode, 1964;* Harmondsworth, Penguin, 1975; New York, Viking, 1964

FP *Four Plays* London, Eyre and Spottiswoode, 1965;* New York, Viking, 1966; South Melbourne, Sun Books, 1967

SM *The Solid Mandala* London, Eyre and Spottiswoode, 1966;* Jonathan Cape, Uniform Edition, 1976; Harmondsworth, Penguin, 1975; New York, Viking, 1966 and 1974; Avon Books, 1975

Viv *The Vivisector* London, Jonathan Cape, 1970;* Harmondsworth, Penguin, 1974; New York, Viking, 1970 and 1974; Avon Books, 1975

ES *The Eye of the Storm* London, Jonathan Cape, 1973;* Harmondsworth, Penguin, 1976; New York, Viking, 1974; Avon Books, 1975

C *The Cockatoos* London, Jonathan Cape, 1974;* New York, Viking, 1975

Introduction

The subject matter of Patrick White's novels is at the same time most
familiar and most strange to the average reader. It is familiar because
White records the private thoughts, secret trials and intimate
emotions of the inner life with almost frightening understanding and
accuracy. His observations on the nature and processes of the
emotional life are universally recognizable and applicable. It is
strange because these observations are often attached to the lives of
the outsider, the afflicted, the genius or the elect—characters who
have their being in a world that is beyond the compass of what we are
pleased to call 'normality'. Equally, his creation or evocation of
external Australian reality in both its natural and its social modes is
familiar to the antipodean who is acquainted with the forms of its
landscape and the cadences of its social voice, but is strange, alluring
and possibly alarming to the overseas reader. But even inside the zone
where White's writing is, or should be, familiar, there is a further element of strangeness or mystery that makes his work stand apart from
the secular tradition of psychological, natural or social realism.
Patrick White has taken the language of the familiar and injected into
it a sense of the arcane and the esoteric that transforms his words into
the hieroglyphs of a vision that may be disquieting to those reared in a
predominantly secular society. The familiar is fused with the strange
to transform the map of Australia and the topography of the inner life
into a realm of myth. That which is known and rational is used in the
service of the unknown and the non-rational.

This book applies itself to the latter aspect of Patrick White's
writings. It is written for those who, like the present writer, have been
intrigued and baffled by the non-rational elements in White's books,
and who find it useful to have some kind of guiding line when
entering the unknown. It is offered as an interpretative scheme that
has emerged from close and repeated readings of the novels. It is not
suggested that White himself began his writing career with such an

organized belief system in mind. This book attempts to extrapolate from White's work a religious pattern that underlies his artistic universe. It sets out in discursive form certain spiritual principles that are latent or implied in his books. It is necessarily systematic, but I have tried as much as possible to let the system grow organically rather than to impose it from outside. I did not begin with any one body of doctrine in mind but tried to express as coherently and accurately as possible the religious beliefs, whatever their source, that Patrick White has woven into the texture of his writing. My approach is more intimately related to Christianity than to any other single creed as White appears to have closer affinities with this than with other religions. But if White is a Christian (and this is by no means certain) his Christianity is not orthodox, and readers must be prepared for departures from accepted Christian dogmas. White has clothed his religious sensibility in garments borrowed from many cultures, chosen according to the needs of his art and message. The analytical scheme offered in the following pages attempts to be as comprehensive as possible. White's range of mythical and cultural reference is too wide, his spiritual and psychological awareness too deep, to be bound in by any one body of doctrine.

I have, however, unblushingly used such terms as 'incarnation', 'redemption', 'rebirth' and 'grace', even though they may have become etiolated in the hands of theologians and may give offence to the rationalist; it appeared pointless constantly to employ periphrastic evasions for what are, in fact, the key issues. White's writing is an attempt to revivify certain theological clichés and to reveal their contemporary human relevance. His awareness of the dilemma of the Word made Flesh is at the heart of his novels, as the discussion in this book attempts to demonstrate. I hope that my employment of apparently conventional terms will not detract from the complexity of this awareness. Where such terms appear they are used flexibly, since it is their inner, not their dogmatic, significance that is in question. A brief quotation from Gabriel Marcel will highlight my intentions:

I realise perfectly that the words 'grace' and 'salvation' give some of you a heartbreaking feeling of staleness. There is nothing new in them for voice or vision. The air around them has been breathed so long that it has become stifling . . . But two observations are necessary here. Grace and salvation are no doubt commonplaces, like their peers, birth, love and death. They can none of them be tricked out anew, for they are all unique. The first time a man falls in love, or knows that he is to be a father or to die, he cannot feel he is hearing stale news. He would more likely feel that it was the first time anyone had ever loved or had a child or prepared for death. It is the same with genuine religious life. Sin, grace and salvation, as words, may be old stuff; as facts they are not, since they lie at the very heart of our destiny.[1]

From time to time I have inevitably had recourse to other thinkers to find clarification or parallels for White's thought. As far as possible I have tried to limit myself to writers who, through my communications with Patrick White, I am reasonably certain have been artistically stimulating to this author. Even here, however, I have made only sparing use of quotations since one cannot be absolutely certain, except in the case of a few direct borrowings, which part of their message has been directly influential. The writers in question are Simone Weil, Jacques Maritain, C. G. Jung, Gabriel Marcel, T. S. Eliot, Martin Buber, Gershom Scholem and the author of the anonymous *Cloud of Unknowing*. I have also made use, with less confidence that White has read them, of R. D. Laing's theories of the origins of schizophrenia as found in *The Divided Self*, and analytical tools borrowed from *Anatomy of Criticism* by Northrop Frye. Broadly speaking these writers—with the exception perhaps of the last two—share a common consciousness with White which is based on their awareness of the intimate but not indissoluble conjunction of essence and existence within the human personality. They express the soul's necessity, while it is in the body, to enter into open dialogue with the created, phenomenal world and all the beauty and misery that it contains. But while they acknowledge, even celebrate, the entanglement with the flesh, they know that there is a mystery of Being running through the material world, upon which mystery existence is ultimately contingent. It is this latter awareness that distinguishes Jung from Freud, Marcel from the author of *The Divided Self* and Patrick White from novelists such as Jean-Paul Sartre.

The approach that I have adopted has forced me to neglect many areas of interest or importance in White's works. I have already mentioned that this is intended as a purely thematic study so that all qualitative judgements, positive or negative, have been suppressed. I have not attempted to analyse the artistic sources of the power and beauty of the writing or the places where this power and beauty fail. Also for thematic reasons I have taken the entire oeuvre as my unit of study. This necessarily involves disregard for developments, changes in emphasis and alterations of style and form. Such a change or development can be seen in the movement away from the psychological realism of the early novels through the mounting religious crescendo of the middle period and back again to the more orthodox mode of *The Vivisector* and *The Eye of the Storm*. But although the method I am using blurs such distinctions, I feel it is justifiable and rewarding to regard the oeuvre as one organic whole, the expression of a single religious and artistic sensibility. Characters, images, situations and themes are repeated so insistently that they must surely be constant and unchanging components of White's temperament and world-view. He seems, in fact, to invite the reader to regard the various works as different manifestations of the same continuous vision by the way he links them together into an unbroken chain. Each novel contains a seed that unfolds in time to become the dominant preoccupation of the next. Holstius, the 'tree walking' of *The Aunt's Story*, grows into The Tree of Man. Stan Parker's lonely vigils in stony places are transformed into Voss's obsession with the desert. The Comet that appears at the end of *Voss* emerges as the Chariot in the next novel, and its fourfold conjunction of the Riders surrounded by the Whirlwind is, in turn, metamorphosed into the key symbol of *The Solid Mandala*. Arthur Brown's passing reference in this novel to 'the Viviseckshunist' swells into Hurtle Duffield's Vivisector, while the 'Mad Eye' that Hurtle paints as a boy becomes the growing point of *The Eye of the Storm*. As well as these overt signs of continuity we find explicit thematic utterances in the early novels illuminating obscure corners of the later ones, while symbols and concepts that have risen to consciousness in the later works organize and elucidate in retrospect much that was only latent in the earlier years. In spite of the manifold forms into which Patrick White has incarnated his vision, there has been no basic change of direction.

Another area that I have avoided, although it is endlessly fascinating, is the hunt (sometimes a wild goose chase) for sources and influences. I have made the study as centripetal as possible and have not attempted to document at length the iconographic history of the Chariot, the philosophic history of the problem of good and evil, or the influences of White's literary forbears. In every chapter, I touch upon subjects of which the ramifications would be endless if explored in detail. I have tried to keep as close to the texts as possible and have not attempted to use White as a starting-point for a discussion of cultural history.

The structure of this book is straightforward. In Part One, I discuss certain philosophical abstractions such as 'evil' and 'time'. These are related to a three-stage cycle of descent and return that underlies the Incarnation. Part Two, which deals with the self, has a mandalic structure of which the centre is the double-natured soul and the outer limit is society. Part Three is concerned with the natural world and the images and symbols that it provides. I have used here a five-level system of exegesis that is similar in some ways to mediaeval schemes of biblical analysis. The three parts overlap considerably, and bare, opaque or unsubstantiated assertions in the earlier pages will be clarified by a process of amplification.

PART ONE

THE WORLD OF BEING

1

The Hidden God and the Incarnation

THE THREE STAGES

The central premise from which the argument of this book unfolds is that behind the appearances of the material world there is a Hidden God. This is the En-Sof of the Kabbalists, or the God celebrated in the mediaeval text *The Cloud of Unknowing*.[2] He is unknown and unknowable; He is pure intensity without extension. He never actually appears in White's pages although nothing there is explicable without an act of faith in His reality. But White is first and foremost a novelist and as such his chief concern is with human existence, not with gnosis. He does not attempt, like Swedenborg, Boehme, or even Blake, to pierce the veil and reveal the hidden processes of the Deity. To the extent that these are mentioned in the following pages it is only as a prologue for the human drama that is being acted out under His inscrutable gaze. It is in man's spiritual predicament, not in theosophy, that White is particularly interested. He shows his characters struggling within the limitations of their existence to understand the destiny that God has imposed upon them. Through their emotional responses and the assumptions of their cultures they try to comprehend the nature of the Hidden God. But no emotion is intense or pure enough, no myth large enough to encompass Him. The speculations and approximations of White's characters, like those of Job and his comforters, always fall short of the truth.

This is not to say that God is completely remote from His creation. On the contrary, every aspect of the world of experience bears His signature. Every encounter in the human and the natural worlds is potentially a moment of dialogue between the individual and God. A strong current of Grace flows through the universe, which may be experienced in the various spiritual principles to be discussed in Part

One, as the spark of divinity placed in the heart of man, which is the subject of Part Two, or in the beauty and terror of the natural world as outlined in Part Three. Union with the Hidden God is not achieved in White's novels by withdrawal from the things of the senses, but by acquiescence to all the conditions of the fallen world in which man finds himself. It is this that distinguishes White from the 'orthodox' mystic. It is strongly suggested in all the books that man may achieve union with the One, but this is only reached through a lifetime of en-counters with a series of Moment Gods, between which encounters vast tracts of desert must be crossed. It is his experience of the desert, as well as of the moments of Grace, that finally brings man to salvation.

So Patrick White's central subject is not the Hidden God but the Incarnation. His novels are an attempt to inject new and urgent meaning into the almost moribund theological doctrine of 'the Word made Flesh'. His work has an underlying metaphysical structure that is given its clearest expression by Laura Trevelyan in *Voss*:

'How important it is to understand the three stages. Of God into man. Man. And man returning into God. Do you find, Doctor, there are certain beliefs a clergyman may explain to one from childhood onwards, without one's un-derstanding, except in theory, until suddenly, almost in spite of reason, they are made clear . . .' (V p. 411)

White's novels explore the implications of the descent of the soul into matter, the plight of the incarnated soul separated from its source, and the return by Grace, at the end of the cycle, to God. This pattern has structured Western metaphysical thinking since its very origins. It can be found in early solar and vegetation myths, and in the stories of Tammuz, Osiris, Dionysus and Orpheus. It has been elaborated into complex and arcane systems by Gnostics, Kabbalists, Platonists and Neo-Platonists. It has provided a spiritual programme for Renaissance painters like Botticelli and Romantic poets like William Blake. In our time it has been given a metapsychological re-interpretation by C. G. Jung. Above all it finds expression in the legend of Christ which combines in a unique way fertility cults and Dionysus worship, the Leda myth, Platonic philosophy, Jewish monotheism and historical fact. White seems to have a temperamen-tal affinity with this 'perennial philosophy' that makes itself felt in every novel.

The pattern of the three stages is used flexibly but the main features remain constant. That which is Above must descend to that which is

Below, the Word must enter the Flesh, in order that the one may be fulfilled, the other may be redeemed. The soul can only embrace God by embracing the created world. Jung expresses the necessity of the descent in the following metaphor:

We stand on a peak of consciousness, believing in a childish way that the path leads upward to yet higher peaks beyond. That is the chimerical rainbow bridge. In order to reach the next peak we must first go down into the land where the paths begin to divide.[3]

Any attempt to avoid the descent, to fly upwards before the conditions of the lower world have been understood and experienced, will end, as with Icarus, in disaster.

In the most general terms the nature of the Above can be outlined as follows. It is one, single and undivided. It is masculine, virgin and paradoxically innocent. It is dry, sterile, brittle and devoid of sensuous content. It holds itself aloof from contaminating contact with the flesh, from the carnal relationships that contain both passion and compassion. It is, or seeks to be, perfect and self-sufficient, master by Will of its own destiny, owing no allegiance to a higher Necessity. This emphasis on will and self-assertion may be so strong that it creates a desire for disentanglement from the material world that leads to actual or metaphorical suicide.

The lower world reverses these attributes. It is the many, the 'ten thousand things', the teeming, fecund world of generation and decay. It is female, moist and rich with sensuous and sensual content. It is contingent, imperfect, and contains a flaw or disease that expresses itself through evil, suffering and death. It is subject to the laws of necessity. It yearns for the descent and embrace of the Above by which it may be liberated. Because of its disease, however, this embrace may inflict a lethal wound on the Above. Paradoxically, it is only by receiving this wound that the higher principle can fulfil its destiny.

There are a great number of cosmogonic myths underlying this pattern, but White's interests are existential rather than gnostic. He is concerned with the human meaning of this conjunction rather than its cosmic origins. Another quotation, again from Jung, will serve to suggest the kind of creation myth that underpins the psychic processes of the novels:

Nous . . . rends the circle of the spheres and leans down to earth and water [i.e. he is about to project himself into the elements]. His shadow falls upon the earth, but his image is reflected in the water. This kindles the love of the elements, and he himself is so charmed with the reflected image of divine beauty that he would fain take up his abode within it. But scarcely has he set foot upon the earth when Physis locks him in a passionate embrace.[4]

Although White himself does not employ them, the terms 'Nous' and 'Physis' have been borrowed from this quotation and used throughout the rest of the book. They express a dualism which in different places could also be rendered as *'animus'* and *'anima'*, 'mind' and 'body', 'Mind' and 'Matter', 'the Word' and 'the Flesh', 'the conscious' and 'the unconscious', or even 'male' and 'female'. (In the last case one must bear in mind that a female character such as Laura Trevelyan may be dominated at times by the Nous principle, while a male character like Arthur Brown may have much of Physis about him.)

White is concerned with the ethical, psychological, artistic and spiritual significance of the descent of Nous to Physis. The descent is an ethical imperative, since it is only by accepting the flesh in all its imperfection that the virtues of compassion and humility can be discovered. It is a psychological necessity since neurosis and psychic disintegration result from locking the self up in the cell of the conscious mind. It is an artistic necessity—the artist's subject is life and by turning his back on life he turns his back on his vocation. Finally, the descent is essential for the soul, which finds God not by fasting, meditation and detachment, but by entering into dialogue with the material world and its creatures.

The cycle of descent and return is in many ways similar to the theme of 'innocence and experience' as found in the nineteenth-century novel, but its goal is not secular wisdom based upon social and emotional maturity (for maturity can often be an enemy of spiritual growth) but redemption. White's most important literary ancestor in this respect is William Blake. It is important to stress the upward turn, the action of Grace, that ends the cycle. White is not 'Lawrentian' although he endorses some of Lawrence's values. He is certainly no antinomian, even if at times—particularly in *The Cockatoos*—he appears close to it. Certainly he celebrates every aspect of the created world, including its flaws, and can sometimes be as Viscous, Sticky or Filthy as anything that Sartre could envisage. But fleshly existence is never an end in itself for White. Thelma Parker in *The Tree of Man* has a thin soul through her fear of human appetites, but her brother Ray, by eating too greedily, becomes spiritually bloated. Carnality may be one expression of the religious instinct but it is never the whole story. The story is only finished when the soul, having unfolded into the world and tasted its fruit, is once more infolded into the One.

This outline may appear too general and abstract to be useful when looking at any particular novel. In the rest of this section an attempt will be made to put some colour into its cheeks by showing how even in its general form it structures and directs the thematic progress of the individual works.

The Living and the Dead and the play *The Ham Funeral* contain biographical hints, such as their setting in Ebury Street where White lived before the war, that suggest they are close to the temperamental roots of his interest in the pattern of descent and ascent. The two young crypto-artists Elyot Standish and the Young Man are dominated by the Nous side of their natures, shut away in their arid upstairs rooms from the sordid but fecund life going on in the streets or in the basement. Their problem is to pass from stage one to stage two of the cycle by descending to, and identifying with, the sleazy reality that repels them. In both the novel and the play, the hero's withdrawal from and struggle with Physis occupies the greater part of the action, and only at the very end are Elyot and the Young Man, having accomplished the difficult descent, able to walk out as full human beings into the stream of life.

The tri-partite structure of *The Aunt's Story* clearly reflects the pattern we are discussing. The quotations with which White introduces the three movements of this literary concerto are themselves revealing evidence:

> Part One: *She thought of the narrowness of the limits within which a human soul may speak and be understood by its nearest of mental kin, of how soon it reaches that solitary land of the individual experience, in which no fellow football is ever heard.* Olive Schreiner.

> Part Two: *Henceforward we walk split into myriad fragments, like an insect with a hundred feet, a centipede with soft-stirring feet that drinks in the atmosphere; we walk with sensitive filaments that drink avidly of past and future, and all things melt into music and sorrow; we walk against a united world, asserting our dividedness. All things, as we walk, splitting with us into a myriad iridescent fragments. The great fragmentation of maturity.* Henry Miller.

> Part Three: *When your life is most real, to me you are mad.* Olive Schreiner.

In Part One, Theodora Goodman is progressively alienated from all human attachments and commitments, an alienation that she partly causes herself, through her pursuit of something she thinks of as 'purity of being'. In Part Two, she temporarily abandons this quest and launches herself whole-heartedly into a multiple fantasy involvement with the bizarre figments of the Hotel du Midi. Through this fragmentation of herself she experiences and lives out all the relationships and emotions with their implications of love and hate, joy and sorrow, that she had been denied or denied herself in Part One. In Part Three, having exorcized all the troubling daemons of her past, Theodora once more detaches herself from the flesh of relationships and continues her search for a way to become most truly herself—a search which looks very much like madness. Her case, like that of Elyot Standish, will be examined in more detail in later chapters. It is worth noting at this point that for Elyot, the Young Man and Theodora Goodman, stage three of the cycle has only guardedly religious implications. The self that they discover or create is a phenomenological, not a spiritual entity. It is still essentially tied to the on-going life of the body.

In *The Tree of Man*, the pattern can be seen in the movement of the novel as a whole and also in the series of minor incidents through which it develops. There are several significant occasions in which Stan Parker experiences the three stages in rapid succession: a sense of strength, ownership and self-confidence is followed by an awareness of weakness, humility and helplessness which, in turn, leads to a sense of impending revelation:

He half-closed his eyes to the sun, and knew that he owned the horse and the buggy, and even the woman and the two children beside him . . . (TM p. 122)

Stan Parker, the father, was trying to recapture the sense of ownership that he had experienced on the journey to the church but now . . . he was less sure. He was uncertain even of his own boots . . . Simultaneously with this pleasing nakedness, the flow of words, the flesh of relationships, were becoming secondary to a light of knowledge. He held up his face to receive he did not know what gift. (TM pp. 123–4)

Stan's whole life exemplifies this same movement, from a period in which he was creator and owner of his farm and everything was 'in his hands', through a growing sense of inadequacy and impotence which corresponds with the time of his wife's mounting flood of illicit sexuality, to a final revelation, by which he becomes aware of the true nature of his divinity.

In *Voss*, Stan Parker's mild, pastoral pretensions to divinity are magnified into the blaring assertions of the deluded German. The arid and painful middle years of the Parkers change into the demonic heat of the desert, and the third stage, that of man returning to God, is heralded by the historic appearance of the Comet. The action in *Voss* is on a grander scale, and the pastoral world which predominates in the former novel is now reduced to Rhine Towers which provides only a brief respite during Voss's agonized progress towards damnation. The name of Nietzsche seems to beg for recognition in a discussion of *Voss*, but in spite of its rather vague evocative power this name will be resisted in the following pages. There are a plethora of Romantic heroes whose fustian, if not Faustian, hybris dates from Voss's own epoch; there is no need to invoke an anachronism. Furthermore, Voss's author, unlike the man who spawned the Superman, has a delightful sense of humour. Although *Voss* is one of the most powerful post-war novels, its power is not augmented by chanting such names as 'Lucifer', 'Faust', 'Nietzsche' or even 'Hitler'. The *übermensch* is never kicked in the stomach by a mule—Voss is.

In *Voss*, the necessity of the descent is expressed largely through images of sexual union. 'Marriage' is a dominant motif in this novel, whether it is the superficial unions of the squatters and merchants, the strange hallucinated relationship between Voss and Laura, the marriage within the psyche of the *animus* and *anima*, or the yearning of the soul for its Lover, Jesus. This imagery even extends to nature, suggesting the cosmic union of Light with Matter:

. . . the surface of a striped mirror, or beaded stool, or some object in cut glass bred triumphantly with the lustier of those beams which entered through the half-closed shutters. (V p. 11)

In those eyes the hills and valleys lay still, but expectant, or responded in ripples of leaf and grass, dutifully, to their bridegroom the sun, till all vision overflowed with the liquid gold of complete union. (V p. 165)

Laura Trevelyan begins the novel as a prig and a rationalist, proud of her self-sufficiency, filled with fascinated revulsion for the coarse bodies of her servants and the ugly, hostile land. She becomes aware of her moral flaws through contact with Voss's hybris, of which her own is a pallid shadow, and resolves to overcome her disgust for the world of the flesh. Her campaign of self-improvement is an exercise of the will, but whereas Voss is trying to will himself out of the body, Laura wills herself into it, by embracing, literally as well as figuratively, her pregnant servant Rose. Rose is the personification of the lower, elemental aspect of Laura herself, just as Laura gives a face to Voss's *anima*. She is also, by implication and image, the spirit of Australia itself. She is ugly, deformed, inarticulate, brown and monotonous, capable only of breeding and suffering. She is totally female, Physis, the deep bass note of the universe. Through her, Laura is born into the physical world, and learns first its joy and then its suffering. Having gained the wisdom of the body, she passes, through the deaths of Rose and Voss, to the wisdom of the dissolution of the body. In the closing chapters of the book we find her in the third stage, detached once more, resisting attempts to involve her in what is finished. In many external ways her condition is now similar to that of the opening chapters, but the difference between the prig and the saint is measured by the amount of love and suffering undergone.

Voss's career is best understood as a struggle between the Nous and Physis principles within his own nature. He is a sick man rather than a sinner, yearning desperately for the material world, but terrified of love and suffering. He wants to mortify and destroy his body, using the harsh landscape of the interior to scrape away his female nature, so that his upper self can be released. He is almost monastic by temperament, but his monasticism is perverse and deluded. Laura, however, activates his lower self, and having accepted her companionship he finds himself increasingly threatened by his own femininity. All men are spiritual hermaphrodites, but this is a truth which Voss struggles fiercely to resist:

> The nurture of faith . . . was an occupation for women . . . Then, there were the few men who assumed humility without shame. It could well be that, in the surrender to selflessness, such individuals enjoyed a kind of voluptuous transport. Voss would sometimes feel embittered at what he had not experienced, even though he was proud not to have done so. How they merge themselves with the concept of their God, he considered almost with disgust. These were the feminine men . . . from . . . whom he must always hold himself aloof, to whom he would remain coldly unwedded. (V p. 52)

> He was no Moslem. His trousers were not designed for parturition. I am One he protested, forming the big O with his convinced mouth. (V p. 287)

Ironically, the more he denies the material world for which he longs, the stronger and more persistent its claims become. He refuses almost to the end to accept it voluntarily, and is taken prisoner by its chthonic inhabitants. Only then does he accept his human status, his wounds and his need for love, and from his trapped and helpless condition cry out to Christ like the feminine men he had despised:

> '*O Jesus*', he cried, '*rette mich nur! Du Lieber!*' Of this too, mortally frightened, of the arms, or sticks, reaching down from the eternal tree . . . (V p. 415)

For Voss the third stage is a combination of Christian and aboriginal eschatology, suggested by Frank Le Mesurier's poem:

> O God, my God, I pray that you will take my spirit out of this my body's remains, and after you have scattered it, grant that it shall be everywhere, and in the rocks, and in the empty water-holes, and in true love of all men, and in you, O God, at last. (V pp. 316–17)

If we step back from *Riders in the Chariot*, we can see it as a vast triptych. The left panel is dominated by Mary Hare's Pleasure Dome and garden, or pseudo-paradise. The central panel is the Infernal Pit whose darkness is illuminated by the tongues of fire from Friedensdorf, Alf Dubbo's Fiery Furnace and Himmelfarb's burning house. The right, or anagogic, panel contains the Chariot of redemption. Closer up, the details, such as those of Mordecai Himmelfarb's life, begin to emerge. Himmelfarb progresses towards his final apotheosis in paint through a series of wave-like motions, each beginning with pretensions to power which, though tempered with self-conscious humility, are no less presumptuous than those of Voss, each declining into a state of chaos and darkness, and each being resolved by a surprising and unpremeditated upward turn. The first of these cycles begins in childhood when there were muted suggestions that the young Mordecai might be a *zaddik*. The early promise is disrupted by a Joycean interlude of sensuality and cynicism, but is restored by his return to the faith and his marriage with Reha. The second epoch, that begins with this marriage, finds Himmelfarb not altogether rejecting the role of the Messiah that has been thrust upon him by his wife and community; but his desertion of his wife and his race on the very night that they need him most throws him into an infernal pit of which Friedensdorf is but the external expression. Saved up from the fire of the extermination camp for future agony, he once more moves towards the light as he travels back to the Promised Land. But in Palestine the promises are not fulfilled, at least for Mordecai, and a third cycle begins when he emigrates to Australia where a pillar of fire—perhaps ironic—rises up to greet him from the tarmac. Once again there is a period of early joy and sensed power, although this time Himmelfarb bends all his will to subjugate his spiritual arrogance. And again there is the downward movement, the disappointments, the failures, that culminate in the botched act of expiation on the tree behind Rosetree's factory. It is at this moment of failure and despair, the lowest trough, that the last upward climb begins, of which the destination, as suggested by Alf Dubbo's paintings, is union with God.

Waldo Brown in *The Solid Mandala* is a case history of the psychic fragmentation and disintegration that result from adhering grimly to the upper principle. Waldo holds tenaciously and neurotically to the myth of his superiority, masculinity and self-sufficiency. Nourishing himself on compensation fantasies and literary aspirations, he shuns and fears all involvement with meaningful human relationships, all participation in the condition of humanity. He is filled with fear of, and longing for, the female principle and the taint that clings to it (the 'pox' which crops up so often in his thoughts). Like Voss, the more he hacks away the flesh of relationships, the more he is caught by the power of Physis. He clings to his belief in his pure 'crystal core' but is compulsively scatological; he asserts his masculinity, but is possessed by the ghost of his mother in a transvestite ritual. He rejects God and is devoured by his own dogs ('dog' being 'god' in reverse). Unlike Voss he dies unredeemed. Voss, through the compulsion of Laura, had submitted to the implications of the descended condition before he died. Waldo, when faced with these implications by Arthur, cannot accept; Arthur's message destroys, rather than saves him:

> 'my heart is bleeding for the Viviseckshunist
> Cordelia is bleeding for her father's life
> all Marys in the end bleed
> but do not complane because they know
> they cannot have it any other way.' (SM p. 212)

Arthur, however, has the spiritual range to be able to encompass both the One and the Many, symbolized on the one hand by the sun, and on the other by the icebergs and moon, that appear at the beginning, middle and end of his life:

Then suddenly he noticed for the first time without strain, it seemed, the red gold disc of the sun. (SM p. 215)

Only in sleep the icebergs moaned, and jostled one another, crunching and tinkling. The moons of sky-blue ice fell crashing silently down to splinter into glass balls which he had gathered in his protected hands. (SM p. 218)

He danced the disc of the orange sun above the icebergs, which was in a sense his beginning, and should perhaps be his end. (SM p. 266)

For Arthur the orange disc had not moved noticeably since he began his upward climb. It was the accompaniment which confused, by its increase in complexity; the groanings, and tinkling and splintering of invisible icebergs. (SM p. 315)

Arthur's life work is to penetrate the opacity of matter and the darkness of his mind, acquainting the light with the love and suffering inherent in the fallen world, and raising the unconscious to the level of the light.

Arthur's chance reference to 'the Viviseckshunist' is taken up as the dominant motif of *The Vivisector*. This is the most 'drowned' of White's novels, existing in the domain of the moist and vegetative. Like Blake, White uses images of the slimy, sticky, viscous and filthy—semen, faeces, honey stains or cold fat—as emblems of the fallen world. There is a rhythm in this novel, suggesting a progressive involvement in experience and guilt, that ends, however, in a final disentanglement from the stickiness of matter. This rhythm of decline is carried forward by the movement of each chapter. Each begins with a new start, a new hope, the potentials of new relationships. Each degenerates into chaos and guilt. Hurtle is increasingly implicated in the evil of the Vivisector, but it is only through these cycles of hope and despair, innocence and experience, that his destiny as an artist and his awareness of the true nature of God can develop. Every collapse is followed by a rebirth, and as he sinks deeper, he is reborn onto higher planes of awareness. At the end, nadir and zenith coincide with a moment of pure Grace as he dies.

The Eye of the Storm is divided into two unequal sections, the dividing line falling between Chapter Five and Chapter Six. The first section takes place over exactly twenty-four hours, the second over several weeks. The pattern of descent and return appears in both parts. In the first section, Elizabeth Hunter is at the centre of her own private maelstrom, being sucked down into the depths of dream or memory, first through her acts of adultery and then to the central trauma of her life—her experience of her husband's final illness and death. During this latter period she comes face-to-face both with her own destructive handiwork and with the suffering and imperfection that is at the heart of the material world she had always been able to dominate. At the end of Chapter Five she is released from her dream-tormented depths and comes shooting back to the surface which is bathed in a numinous light of roses. This Grace or release of rose light is only a temporary respite, a new peak from which an even deeper descent will begin:

Sister de Santis only gave herself time to stuff the roses by thorny handfuls in an old washstand jug left over in the mahogany bathroom before she hurried in. At the same time, the relic in her charge was tossed up out of whatever infernal depths, and stranded on the shores of consciousness.

... the roses sparkled drowzed brooded leaped flaunting their earthbound flesh in an honourably failed attempt to convey the ultimate.

'Yes—our roses,' Elizabeth Hunter repeated.

Which Mary de Santis interpreted as: we, the arrogant perfectionists or pseudo-saints, shall be saved up out of our shortcomings for future trial. (ES pp. 210–11)

In the second and longer section of the novel, Mrs Hunter is forced to face an even greater trauma than the death of her husband—the prospect of her own at the hands of her children. She is given the grace or strength to bear this last trial by her memory of her experience on Brumby Island. This experience, too, is organized around the pattern of the three stages. In the first, Elizabeth Hunter is supremely, if diffidently, conscious of her own power and magnificence. As the storm bursts, her sense of her own worth and beauty is replaced by a devastating awareness of the corruption and moral pus that has been collecting in her diseased conscience. But persevering, by luck, strength or Grace, through the worst awfulness of the storm, she is finally granted her moment in the Eye, which is a fleeting encounter with the Hidden God.

This brief review raises as many questions as it answers; these questions will be explored in greater detail in the course of this book. The main purpose of this discussion has been to establish a basic pattern to be kept in mind during the course of the following analyses.

THE PRINCIPLE OF ANTINOMY

As the One, the Hidden God, emanates from His secret source into the world of extension, He expresses Himself through a series of paired principles such as good and evil, joy and suffering, or life and death. These become the laws of necessity which govern the fallen world, and to which man must accept his subjection. Although known chiefly by their manifestations in human thought and action, they have an existence prior to and higher than the individual. They are Ideas, not ideas, which run through the material world as electricity runs through wire. It is an essential part of man's spiritual destiny that he should become aware of, and enter into relationship with, these principles, just as he must enter into relationships with the more concrete aspects of the phenomenal world. They are expressions of God, and by trying to evade them man also evades God's destiny.

An extremely important aspect of White's world-view, one that we shall return to in Part Three, is the idea of antinomy. No principle, emotion, action or image is unambiguous in its implications. There is an ambivalence in everything, so that redemption or disintegration can flow from the same source. This antithetical quality is itself part of the purpose of God. Joy and suffering, life and death, good and evil, and love and hate work together to a higher end. Neither side is sufficient in itself. White records the simultaneous demands of opposite forces in a cyclical rhythm through which they alternate and complete one another. In the words of Martin Buber:

Man's religious situation, his *being there* in the Presence, is characterised by its essential and indissoluble antinomy . . . He who wishes to carry through the conflict of the antinomy other than with his life transgresses the significance of the situation. The significance of the situation is that it is lived and nothing but lived, continually, ever anew, without foresight, without forethought, without prescription, in the totality of its antinomy.

. . . I am compelled to take both to myself, to be lived together, and in being lived they are one.[5]

White's awareness of the importance of these abstract principles is suggested by his choice of epigraphs for his first two novels. The quotation from Gandhi in *Happy Valley* and from Helvétius in *The Living and the Dead* both refer to 'a law' or 'principles' which govern the human condition. In the Helvétius quotation paired opposites are explicitly referred to

Je te mets sous la garde du plaisir et de la douleur;
l'un et l'autre veilleront à tes pensées, à tes actions;
. . . et . . . te découvriront un jour les principes simples,
au développement desquels sont attachés l'ordre et le
bonheur du monde moral.

At the end of *The Aunt's Story*, there is both a conceptual and an imagistic expression of the eternal co-existence of thesis and antithesis. Holstius explains the concept to Theodora Goodman in these terms:

'What is it,' she asked in agony, 'you expect me to do or say?'
'I expect you to accept the two irreconcilable halves . . .'

'You cannot reconcile joy and sorrow,' Holstius said. 'Or flesh and marble, or illusion and reality, or life and death. For this reason, Theodora Goodman, you must accept . . .' (AS p. 293)

A few pages later the idea is encapsulated in an evocative image, which suggests the cosmic process through which the One, with intensity but no extension, bubbles out into the phenomenal world:

> Presently she went down through the trees to the place where the spring ran. She sat beside the brown water which welled out of the rusty tin, full of frog spawn and the skeletons of leaves. (AS p. 298)

> Out of the rusted tin welled the brown circles of perpetual water, stirring with great gentleness the eternal complement of skeleton and spawn. (AS p. 300)

Riders in the Chariot is almost manichean in its polarisation, structured around the opposition of Good and Evil, with their accompanying apocalyptic or daemonic images of light and dark. In *The Solid Mandala*, the interaction of opposites is highlighted by the use of twins, suggesting the joint actions of *yin* and *yang* through the cosmos and within the psyche. White's dualism appears in *The Eye of the Storm* as the 'dichotomy of earthbound flesh and aspiring spirit' (ES p. 209). This dichotomy is already hinted at in the epigraphs with which he introduces the novel:

> *I was given by chance this human body so difficult to wear.*
> *No* play.

> *Men and boughs break;*
> *Praise life while you walk and wake;*
> *It is only lent.*   David Campbell.

Although the two sides of the antinomy we have suggested here may exist simultaneously, fused into a paradoxical co-existence that White often expresses by adopting an irony of style towards a serious theme or image, there is usually a tendency for thesis to give way to antithesis as stage one moves into stage two, and for both to be blended into a higher synthesis as the end of the cycle is reached. As we have seen in such cases as those of Himmelfarb or Hurtle Duffield, this synthesis may itself be a starting-point for a new cycle which, beginning from a higher point, may well descend to a deeper abyss. In the end, however, no matter how far apart the two sides of the antinomy may appear, they are fused together as joy and suffering are infolded into Joy, love and hate are infolded into Love, life and death are infolded into Life. White's style is generated by the tension of opposites, by the alignment of poles that are not by nature aligned. If reconciliation seems difficult it is because White is trying to express, sometimes through banality, irony or even apparent cynicism, his belief that nature is not the ultimate arbiter of spiritual alignment.

2
Messengers of the Loved One

JOY AND SUFFERING

As the epigraph from Helvétius quoted in the last chapter suggests, the twin principles of joy and suffering (or their various synonyms) are basic components of the groundswell of existence. Only by opening itself fully to both can the descended soul be opened to God. A quotation from Simone Weil may illuminate their role in White's worldview:

In order that a new sense should be formed in us which enables us to hear the universe as the vibration of the word of God, the transforming powers of suffering and of joy are equally indispensable. When either of them comes to us we have to open the very centre of our soul to it, just as a woman opens her door to messengers from her loved one. What does it matter to a lover if the messenger be polite or rough, so long as he gives her a message?[6]

The problem of suffering is met everywhere in White's novels; the quotation from Gandhi used for *Happy Valley* could be used with equal appropriateness for all his works:

It is impossible to do away with the law of suffering which is the one indispensable condition of our being. Progress is to be measured by the amount of suffering undergone ... the purer the suffering the greater is the progress.

This emphasis on suffering, however, must be immediately balanced by stressing the important part that joy plays in White's novels. As though to correct a false emphasis White adds 'le plaisir' to 'la douleur' when he chooses a motto for his second novel. The joy in this book remains purely notional, but in *The Aunt's Story* a rich, sensuous beauty and a warm awareness of human affections enter White's writing. In all the later novels this sense of beauty and warmth is as strong as the action of affliction and desolation. White's 'endorsed' characters are marked off from those around them not only by their capacity for suffering but also by their response to the sensuous world and to the potential for love in others.

When talking of the 'law of suffering' one must distinguish clearly what kind of suffering White has in mind. Physical suffering plays a very minor part in his novels, limited almost entirely to the pain of childbirth which can be seen as a symbol of the pain consequent to the descent of the soul into the flesh. When he speaks of suffering he does not mean physical, or external affliction; consequently he quickly rejected the doctor-hero as a solution to the problem. In modern fiction the doctor has tended to replace the saint or martyr as hero, offering as he does an active rather than a quietist solution to the problem of suffering. The typical figure is Dr Rieux of *La Peste* by Camus. After *Happy Valley* (whose theme, like so many others in White's early writing, pre-dates by many years the preoccupations of post-war European writers), White rejects activist solutions, as embodied in Dr Halliday, and chooses instead the saint, the martyr and the artist as his protagonists. The type of suffering he is examining is an emotional or spiritual malaise not amenable to active solutions.

He is not interested in the large-scale and public suffering that results from great historical upheavals like the War or the Depression, nor in those virtuoso passages of individual suffering which make newspaper headlines. Where these do appear, as in the German section of *Riders in the Chariot* or the Jack Frost and Ray Parker murders, they are important as contexts, symbols or catalysts for the more muted misery which is the real subject. In *Voss*, for example, the obscure suffering of Laura Trevelyan is just as significant as the epic disaster which overtakes the explorers.

Nor does he write about the suffering that results from the slow attrition of poverty and social deprivation. The deprivation with which he is concerned can bite as deeply into the materially prosperous middle class as into the working class. He does not sentimentalize poverty, and is awake to its grinding effects on such families as the Duffields, but at the same time he appreciates that the materially deprived may possess a reality that has been lost by the synthetic souls of the bourgeoisie.

His subject is the suffering that is related to the most intimate affections, aspirations and guilts of the soul, which are almost invisible to the eye of the casual observer. He is concerned with the suffering of ruptured relationships, thwarted affections and failures of communication. He is concerned with the pain and guilt generated within the family, where husbands and wives, children and parents are involved ineluctably in the dual processes of personality creation and personality destruction that constitute family life. A decade before R. D. Laing wrote *The Divided Self*, White was analysing and depicting the slow mental or emotional murder that one member of a family—often a dominant wife or mother—can inflict on others. He shows the claustrophobia and frustrations of intimate relationships, the ambivalence of love and hate, the paradox of the mystery of intimacy which is also the mystery of distance. He shows the suffering of the inner, the emotional life, trying to fulfil itself in the context of the emotional lives of others.

The quotation from Gandhi speaks of the 'progress' which is made through suffering. 'Progress' is obviously a desirable thing, but White is not a monastic masochist, advocating the hairshirt and the bed of nails as necessary spiritual exercises. On the contrary, he shows his characters struggling indignantly against the affront and indignity of the law of suffering. Few of them deliberately seek suffering, and those, like Voss, who do are shown to be spiritually perverse. Most have a healthy sense of outrage at the lot that destiny has cast for them, and fight to retain their right to personal happiness. Suffering creeps upon them unawares in their pursuit of happiness and they learn only with difficulty to submit:

'I shall resist all attempts to make me suffer, or to bring suffering to others,' said the younger woman, to whom it was still a matter of will and theory.

'I did not expect to suffer,' Rose Portion was telling. '. . . I was not meant to suffer, not then, or now—you would have said. But sufferin' creeps up. And in different disguises. You do not recognise it, miss. You will see.' (V. pp. 82–3)

Suffering, it appears, is ubiquitous and unavoidable; everyone must be caught by it sooner or later. One has no choice in the matter, but one does have a choice in the quality of the response. This brings us to Gandhi's 'purity' of suffering. This must be understood not as 'intensity'—a migraine does not have more spiritual value than a hangover—but rather as acquiescence to the law. This point must be made in order to avoid what appears to be a paradox: if suffering brings spiritual progress, and if it is true that suffering is inescapable, then surely everyone must make progress, since everyone must suffer. But White's message is that the law of suffering is effective for regeneration not to the extent that his characters are subject to it, but to the extent that they endorse it, let it slide into the soul and marry the innermost part.

This, in fact, is a rare ability. A large part of the motivation of

White's lesser characters is a drive to avoid spiritual and emotional suffering. He sees a great deal of human behaviour not as a positive impulse to achieve apparent goals but rather as a negative and self-defeating flight from that suffering which Weil calls 'the messenger of the loved one'. He has an observant eye, sometimes sympathetic, sometimes satirical, for the defensive postures which people adopt to ward off this messenger, the contortions of subjects repudiating a law they already obey.

People erect external palisades against the assaults of suffering, using whatever building material comes to hand. Rigid conformity to the class-status system, the adoption of its icons and mores, is essentially a defensive position; social class is used at every level, from the squatocracy to the proletariat, as a system of earthworks thrown up against the messenger of God. Many, like Amy Parker, build defences in human flesh, using love, sex or motherhood as barriers against insecurity and fear. The cultivation of Causes and Great Ideas serves the same purpose: Mrs Courtney's charities, Hero Pavloussi's pilgrimage to Perialos or Palfreyman's participation in Voss's expedition are all evasive rather than affirmative actions.

The mind also has a wide range of inner defence mechanisms. The danger area can be anaesthetized, avoided, forgotten or ignored. Catherine Standish, for example, refuses to think about some unpleasant incidents involving her husband; Waldo Brown represses distressing memories which only bob to the surface years later, and Mary Hare is a master hand at moral amnesia when it comes to the question of certain traumatic deaths. Some characters retreat to the emotional shallows, preferring sentimentality or rational kindness to the deeper waters that contain love and suffering. Others attempt to render suffering impotent by a 'knowingness' which encompasses but cannot respond to it. The contaminating particles of suffering are sometimes expelled in outbursts of rage or hatred so that suffering is passed on to another. Characters attempt to destroy the object that generates suffering, reifying and lampooning it, as does Waldo Brown, or literally exterminating it, as Voss shoots his dog or the Lucky Sevens kill Himmelfarb. Others again turn inward and destroy part or all of themselves, denying their family, their faith, their God, or, as in the case of Theodora Goodman, their own existence.

The important thing about these and the many other defence mechanisms that people adopt is that they are ultimately ineffective and self-defeating. To the extent that they are, or appear, successful, they only open the soul to a higher and more lethal form of suffering. The root of suffering is the separation of the soul from God, its

assumption of an individual identity. For some purpose that remains
unknown it is part of the divine scheme that this assumption of the
flesh should be made. The affliction of the incarnation, of being involved in the imperfection of the fallen world, is a 'messenger of the
loved one' and those who attempt to deny or evade it are also denying
God. The lower forms of suffering bring distress in the short term, but
refusal to accept them leads ultimately not to temporary, but to total
separation from God. The defence mechanisms bring at the very least
spiritual mediocrity, at worst a condition of emotional and spiritual
disintegration which even within time can resemble Hell. This is the
central paradox of the human situation; the basic affliction of
mankind is separation from God, but this distance from God is part
of His scheme, and only by accepting all its consequences can man
finally return to Him.

Having made these general remarks about the law of suffering, we
shall now turn to the pattern of the three stages, to see how it applies
in this particular instance. A quotation from Simone Weil provides a
useful framework for the discussion:

The soul's natural inclination to love beauty is the trap God most frequently
uses in order to win it and open it to the breath from on high . . . This was the
trap which enticed Cora. All the heavens above were smiling at the scent of the
narcissus, so was the entire earth and all the swelling ocean. Hardly had the
poor girl stretched out her hand before she was caught in the trap. She fell into
the hands of the living God. When she escaped she had eaten the seed of the
pomegranate which bound her forever. She was no longer a virgin; she was
the spouse of God.

The beauty of the world is the mouth of a labyrinth. The unwary individual
who on entering takes a few steps, is soon unable to find the opening . . . and if
he does not lose courage, if he goes on walking, it is absolutely certain that he
will finally arrive at the centre of the labyrinth. And there God is waiting to eat
him. Later he will go out again, but he will be changed, he will have become
different, after being eaten and digested by God. Afterwards he will stay near
the entrance so that he can gently push all those who come near into the
opening.[7]

As was mentioned earlier, White's characters do not deliberately
seek out suffering. The early stages of the descent into the world of
matter are usually typified by a sense of innocent happiness. The
characters are attracted to the phenomenal world by its sensuous
beauty, drawn into involvement with others by the promise of love
and personal happiness. In *Voss*, for instance, both Laura and Voss
begin their descent into matter with a sense of great personal hap-

piness. In Chapter Seven, Laura consummates her sympathetic involvement with the pregnancy of Rose Portion in the rose garden which is overflowing with a voluptuous richness. In Chapter Six, the idyllic beauty and serenity of the earthly paradise at Rhine Towers work on Voss to such an extent that he deviates from his own nature so far as to propose to Laura. In *The Vivisector*, as was pointed out in the first chapter, each phase of Hurtle's life opens with an influx of hope and the opening-out of new vistas of sensuous beauty. We find the same early hope for personal happiness during Theodora Goodman's childhood at Meroë and also during the opening days of her stay at the Hôtel du Midi. It is present at the Parkers' farm during their first years of marriage and dominates Himmelfarb's life during the brief epochs of hope that precede the troughs of suffering.

This early happiness is ephemeral; it is a lure to involve the soul in the labyrinths of the created world. It is not a permanent condition. Holstius tells Theodora: 'In fact, you might say that expectation of happiness is expectation of sorrow. The separating membrane is negligible.' (AS p. 292). The early bloom fades as the descent into the world continues. The law of suffering becomes increasingly insistent, the harshness and opposition of matter more obtrusive, as the distance from God increases. As inevitably as the joy of Christmas leads to the events of Good Friday, happiness blows away like pear blossom, leaving only bare sticks behind (V p. 352).

As the action moves towards its resolution, this downward progression deepens into a black night of the soul, an abyss in which the character is plunged totally in matter. The sense of personal power and worth is reduced to nothing, the soul seems absolutely separated from others, from itself and from God. Elyot Standish sits in a state of spiritual torpor, Theodora Goodman runs from her shack like a hunted animal, things pass completely out of the hands of the crippled Stan Parker, and Voss, helpless in the hands of the aborigines, realizes that both his expedition and his pretensions to divinity have failed. Himmelfarb is crucified, but receives no conclusive sign from God, Arthur Brown lies down in a black alley where drunks piss, Hurtle Duffield paints a pitch-black painting—the nadir is reached. Such a black night occurs to Elizabeth Hunter as the cyclone hits Brumby Island:

Perhaps it is you who are responsible for the worst in people. Like poor little Basil sucking first at one unresponsive teat then the other the breasts which will not fill in spite of the nauseating raw beef and celery sandwiches prescribed by Dr Whatever—to 'make milk to feed your baby'. Instead of milk, 'my baby' (surely the most tragic expression?) must have drawn off the pus from everything begrudged withheld to fester inside the breast he was cruelly offered.

This night (morning by the shagreen clock) it is the earth coming to a head: practically all of us will drown in the pus which is gathered in it.

Elizabeth Hunter was almost torn off her shelf by a supernal blast then put back by a huge thrust or settling of exhausted atoms.

She lay and submitted to someone to whom she had never been introduced. Somebody is always tinkering with something. It is the linesman testing for the highest pitch of awfulness the human spirit can endure. (ES pp. 423-4)

More agonizing than the sense of personal powerlessness, pain or guilt which comes to characters at this point is the sense of failure. This is not so much failure in the eyes of the world, as failure to live up to their own ideals, to measure up to their own self-imposed standards. Arthur Brown, for example, dedicates his life to his brother, accepts a mission of love and responsibility for Waldo, in which, at the end, he discovers he has failed totally. Himmelfarb dedicates himself to a life of atonement but paradoxically finds himself constantly the target for other people's efforts to atone, and when his moment of expiation comes at the hands of the Lucky Sevens he is given no indication from above that his sacrifice has been accepted. This is the supreme form of suffering, the greatest distance from God. At this moment of failure man becomes completely subject to the condition of matter, of which the very essence is imperfection and incompleteness. The act of failure is the final acceptance of and symbol for the nature of the lower world. Like everything else failure must be accepted and through this act of acceptance it is redeemed:

'The mystery of life is not solved by success, which is an end in itself, but by failure . . .' (V p. 289)

It seemed to him as though the mystery of failure might be pierced only by those of extreme simplicity of soul, or else by one who was about to doff the outgrown garment of the body. He was weak enough, certainly by now, to make the attempt which demands the ultimate in strength. (RC p. 480)

By a paradox which is fundamental to Christianity, it is at the heart of the earthly labyrinth, the centre of Hell when man is at the greatest distance from God, that he discovers his divinity. It is now that he performs the true *imitatio Christi*, undergoing the same necessity that made Christ cry out: 'My God, my God, why hast Thou forsaken me?' At the lowest point of the descent, when he has arrived at

Calvary, man merges with God.

The suffering that led up to this moment of Grace falls away to be replaced by a new and higher sense of joy—the joy of union. Sometimes this moment of Grace coincides with the moment of death, as in the cases of Stan Parker and Hurtle Duffield. But sometimes it is only a fleeting encounter, a momentary promise that gives the soul the strength to endure the further suffering to which it must be subjected. It is only after the full span of the life sentence has been served that complete union can take place. Premature extinction during a moment of theophany may be a frustration, not a consummation, of man's spiritual destiny; Elizabeth Hunter acknowledges this:

'. . . I was prepared for my life to be taken from me. Instead the birds accepted to eat out of my hands. There was no sign of hatred or fear while we were— encircled. What saved me was noticing a bird impaled on a tree. It must have been blown against the sharp spike left by a branch which had snapped off. I think I was reminded that one can't escape suffering. Though it's only human to try to escape it. So I took refuge. Again, it was the dead bird reminding me the storm might not have passed . . .' (ES p. 409)

But whether the character passes out of the body during such a moment or is saved up for future trials, it is clear that the resolution of the problem of suffering is spiritual rather than philosophical. In White, as in Job, it is not reasoning that pierces the veil but theophany. As in Job the whole problem of suffering simply falls away through direct contact of the soul with God. The only meaning that suffering has is that it makes such contact possible. The moment of Grace casts a light on everything that has led to it and everything that follows it, which illuminates the reason for the endorsement of the law of suffering and the condemnation of those who have tried to evade the messenger of God.

GOOD AND EVIL

At the same time that man is the victim of the universal law of suffering (a law which even God, in the person of Christ, must obey), he is also implicated in the principle of evil through which man and God become agents and inflicters, not victims of suffering. The concept of 'evil' makes its most explicit appearance in *Rider in the Chariot*, but the problem exists by implication in all the novels. Wherever there is suffering there is a human or divine agent, whose motives must be understood. White's characters wrestle with the question of the source of affliction, and according to their temperaments or religions come up with various answers. Himmelfarb regards evil as a subordinate principle which is given power to act by the sins of man in general and the Jews in particular: ' "The sins of Israel have given Sammael the legs on which he now stands." ' (RC p. 161). Hurtle Duffield places the blame squarely on God Himself, whom he imagines as a vicious and arbitrary satrap who torments mankind for sport. Like Job's approximations, any human statement must be partial and inexact, but, again as in Job, it seems certain that the ultimate responsibility must lie with the Deity, at least for tolerating, at most for causing suffering. A full examination of the role of God in the causation of evil has been reserved for the final chapter of the book. In the present section good and evil will be examined in their human aspects.

For White the categories of 'good' and 'evil' are not purely external, ethical concepts, imposed from a moral code upon the inner life of the character. At the human level, good and evil have an intimate, organic relationship with the temperament. The psychological, the ethical and the spiritual grow together from the human heart and cannot validly be separated from one another. White does not annihilate ethical values by reducing all human behaviour to a question of social conditioning or psychological determinism: man is ultimately answerable for his own actions. Nor, however, does he destroy the complexity and subtlety of human compulsion or motivation with the sledge-hammer of morality. He shows the organic connection between psychology and ethics, so that certain inner states will emanate into the world in the form of actions which may be morally flaccid or actively destructive. Habitual patterns of response to life are formed which may adversely affect others but will certainly turn and eat back into the soul. That which begins as frigidity or fear may develop into neurosis and end in psychic disintegration which, in turn, can be figured as a more than metaphorical Hell. Such characters as Mrs Flack or Waldo Brown are not damned by their author, or by God; they generate a moral cancer which destroys them by an almost biological retroactive process. If Grace is denied them it is because they have themselves made the first denial.

The same organic connection can be found existing in the case of goodness, as seen in this quotation from *Riders in the Chariot*:

. . . she would lie there wondering whether she had conceived again in lust. For one so strong, it must be admitted she was regrettably weak. Or else kind . . .

Faith is not less persuasive for its fluctuations. Rather, it becomes a living thing, like a child fluttering in the womb. So Mrs Godbold's faith would stir

and increase inside the grey, gelatinous envelope of morning, until, at last, it was delivered, new-born, with all the glory and confidence of fire.
This almost biological aspect of his wife's faith was what the husband hated most. (RC p. 259)

The source and the end of these almost biological processes are spiritual. The end is either redemption or disintegration. What is the metaphysical source?

The theme of 'sickness' runs through all White's works: his first hero was a doctor, while Hurtle Duffield is, in the words of Rimbaud that introduce *The Vivisector*, 'the Great Invalid'. There is a taint in the created world, and particularly in the nature of man, from which arises much of the evil that man is heir to. The wound from which man suffers has a paradoxical or double-natured origin. It is caused, on the one hand, by his separation from God and his involvement in the imperfect and contingent phenomenal world. In this world he obeys laws of necessity that often dictate an instinctive cruelty which man has in common with the animals. On the other hand, the wound is the kinship of man with God which makes him restless and disaffected with these laws. His disease is simultaneously the distance and the intimacy of God. The absence of God is an affliction, but so is His presence. This dilemma is depicted dramatically in the short story 'Sicilian Vespers' in which Ivy Simpson commits a compulsive act of blasphemy on the floor of San Fabrizio while above her on the ceiling the Christ Pantocrator, so palpable but so distant, weeps (C p. 243). In 'The Night the Prowler', this same sense of distance generates Felicity Bannister's obsessive acts of outrage and culminates in her agonized cry: 'I fuck you, God, for holding out on me!' (C p. 164).

The evil which arises from separation from God, from involvement in identity and ego, expresses itself in acts of cruelty. The motif of 'murder' with its associated images of knives, swords, axes and spears, appears constantly in the novels. There is some impulse in human nature which makes it difficult for most people to refrain from twisting the knife in the wounds of another. This sometimes appears to occur for the most trivial of reasons, out of boredom or petty malice or even from a perverted sense of humour. Brutality may also be a form of self-defence or revenge against someone who, wittingly or unwittingly, has been a cause of suffering. It may also be a necessity that is thrust upon a character who is seeking to escape from an intolerably claustrophobic situation.

Most typically this impulse to brutality flows from the strong to the weak, from the 'normal' to the outsider, the afflicted or the repulsive.

We see this in the persecution of Theodora by Mrs Goodman and, of course, Himmelfarb by Mrs Flack. Simone Weil highlights this facet of human nature in the following alarming observation:

If a hen is hurt, the others rush upon it, attacking it with their beaks. This phenomenon is as automatic as gravitation. Our senses attach all the scorn, all the revulsion, all the hatred which our reason attaches to crime, to affliction. Except for those whose soul is inhabited by Christ, everybody despises the afflicted to some extent, although practically no one is conscious of it.[8]

Behind this compulsion, however, lies a profound ambivalence. Although the strong and normal hate and are repelled by the weak and different, they are at the same time fascinated by them. It is dimly sensed that these outsiders possess some secret gift which those who despise them lack and, probably unknown even to themselves, long for. Most people suffer from a profound spiritual frustration, being estranged from the true source of their own being. The suffering that this causes is turned into hatred of the scapegoat who is loathed not simply for his strangeness but also for his affinity with a reality denied to the normal. Voss's scorn of Palfreyman, Amy Parker's need to wound her husband, Tom Godbold's loathing of his wife, Waldo's profound ambivalence towards Arthur, are all symptoms of this longing.

Cruelty and evil are generated by the suffering caused by spiritual need; suffering is transformed into evil as the victim attempts to transfer it to a scapegoat, until someone appears who will break the chain by taking the full charge into his own body. This receives its most obviously religious expression in the crucifixion of Himmelfarb, in which the frustrated impulse towards God that exists in a secular society expresses itself in the scapegoating of the Jew. The irony of this incident is that, through their obsession with the Christ they have suppressed, the mob's practical joke turns into a re-enactment of the very scene to which their material culture denies significance. As it gains momentum, everyone is swept up into an obsessive and ritual performance. They find themselves playing parts that suddenly reveal to them the truth of the Easter myth, and their actions bite back into their own souls, increasing rather than relieving their suffering:

If some of the spectators suffered the wounds to remain open, it was due probably to an unhealthy state of conscience, which could have been waiting since childhood to break out. For those few, the drops trembled and lived. How they longed to dip their handkerchiefs, unseen.

Others had to titter for a burlesque, while turning aside their faces in an attempt to disguise what they suspected might be blasphemy. (RC pp. 462–3)

If Blue had gone into the plating-shop, and was holding his semblance of a head, it was because he felt real crook. It was the beer. It was the beer. It was the fount of blue and crimson sparks. It was the blood that had not touched his lips, in driest memory, or now. But would, in fact, have turned him up. So that, between longing and revulsion, not to mention the hiccups, he went into a corner, and vomited. (RC pp. 468–9)

The retroactive effect that evil has upon the evil-doer is basic to White's thought on the subject. Cruelty can inflict superficial harm to its object but its real destructive potential works inwardly upon the subject. Evil destroys itself, whether it be an evil passion or a person dominated by an evil passion. The fire at the Hôtel du Midi in *The Aunt's Story* destroys, at one level, all those characters who have been guilty of false or destructive attitudes; at another level, it is the purging of evil passions in Theodora Goodman herself. In *Riders in the Chariot*, the truly evil characters end, by imagistic suggestion, in Hell, while the more venal Mrs Chalmers-Robinson ends in an 'obscure purgatory' (RC p. 545). Waldo Brown dies of his own hatred: '"Waldo can only of died of spite like a boil must burst at last with pus"' (SM p. 317). This idea is given formal expression by Mary Hare:

'Oh, yes, there is evil!' She hesitated. 'People are possessed with it. Some more than others!' she added with force. 'But it burns itself out. Some are even destroyed as it does.' (RC p. 172)

'There is one of the evil ones!' Miss Hare decided to reveal just so much, and to point with a finger. 'How evil, I am not yet sure. But she has entered into a conspiracy with another devil, and will bring suffering to many before it destroys them both.' (RC p. 174)

Evil damns the evil-doer and has a redemptive function for those who are prepared to offer themselves as scapegoats. But the redemptive function of evil—without Iscariot and Pilate, Christ could never have fulfilled His mission on the Cross—raises a question of divine justice that is essentially extraneous to White's novels, but may perturb the modern reader, particularly in *Riders in the Chariot* and *The Solid Mandala*. The justification of evil in terms of its victim is clear: the knives, viewed correctly, are the nails of the Crucifixion and the wounds they inflict lead to redemption. But where is the justice for those who wield the knives? They are God's agents, bringing about the redemption of the elect, but in this very function they themselves are damned. One can only point to this problem, White does not resolve it. The same mystery exists in Christ's words to Judas:

The Son of man goes as it is written of him, but woe to that man by whom the Son of man is betrayed! It would have been better for that man if he had not been born. (Matthew 26:24)

Involvement with the chain of evil, however, goes deeper than a simple division between the bad who perform it and are damned, and the good who suffer it and are redeemed. We must turn now to the problem of the involvement of the elect themselves in the causation of evil. 'Good' and 'evil' are not fixed categories. Like everything else in White, they are twined around each other, complementing and completing their opposite partner. Although White endorses the quality of 'goodness', and does not hesitate to label characters as 'good', or 'honest', it is a limited and limiting virtue. Characters like Joe Barnett, the Johnsons, Stan Parker, Judd, Mrs Godbold and Arthur Brown are 'good' people. They are often associated with simple, honest material things, such as bread, milk, wood, chairs and tables—objects that are close to their raw materials and have the integrity of their function. Such people are essentially innocent, close to their original clay, but their very virtue limits them. They must be opened up through experiencing the taint of matter, or tasting the fruit of the Tree of the Knowledge of Good and Evil. The Fall is a necessary prerequisite for the Resurrection.

This involves an experience of evil, not just as victim, but as agent. Most of White's central characters find themselves actually or potentially inflicting suffering on others.

Theodora Goodman, driven to desperation by her mother, picks up a knife and although the murder is not actually committed, she senses her own complicity in guilt (AS p. 128). Stan Parker suffers from the memory that he never spoke up about the old man he had seen in a tree during the flood and had suspected was drowned (TM p. 302). Palfreyman feels guilty about deserting his sister after denying her the right to kill herself (V p. 292). All four Riders are oppressed by a sense of wrong-doing and betrayal. Mary Hare is involved with a number of mysterious deaths, particularly that of her father; Himmelfarb deserts his wife and community; Ruth Godbold blames herself, or is blamed, for the death of her brother, and Alf Dubbo betrays his paintings to Humphrey Mortimer. The more complicated cases of Voss, Hurtle Duffield and Elizabeth Hunter will be examined shortly.

The case of Arthur Brown brings us to another, and more paradoxical, involvement in evil causation. The cases above are all lapses from an essential goodness, but characters can also be agents of suffering through, not in spite of, their goodness. As was mentioned earlier, certain characters inspire negative emotions in others simply because they exist. They are different, and they possess a certain inner light which the 'normal' cannot tolerate. The good torment the bad into acts of perversity or cruelty by their very existence. This is implicit in all the earlier novels. Mrs Goodman is exasperated into spite by her daughter's plainness and angularity. Stan Parker is, in a sense, very much to blame for his wife's adultery; she is too weak to sustain co-existence with his self-enclosed integrity. Voss is constantly being driven to acts of malice by the goodness and innocence of men like Palfreyman and Judd. Tom Godbold is hounded and harried deeper and deeper into his neurotic hell by the humourless and naïve efforts of his wife to 'save' him, while Mary Hare is guilty of her father's hatred for her and Himmelfarb, through his Jewishness and ugliness, forces Mrs Flack and Mrs Jolley to persecute him. This paradox does not rise to consciousness, however, until *The Solid Mandala*, where Arthur Brown accepts full responsibility for his brother's evil. His love and devotion, operating through the clumsy vehicle of his unfortunate exterior, force Waldo into defensive acts of destruction, which culminate in his death, a suicide which Waldo interprets as murder. Arthur, however, realizes with horror that goodness and innocence are not sufficient, and blames himself for Waldo's death:

> Arthur was afraid Waldo was preparing to die of the hatred he had bred in him. Because he, not Waldo, was to blame. Arthur Brown, the getter of pain. (SM pp. 294–5)

> 'I was the one who should have died,' said Arthur. 'In the beginning. They never told me.'

> 'Only Waldo told me. In the end. When it was too late. I killed him. I killed Waldo in the end.' (SM p. 311)

Voss, Hurtle Duffield and Elizabeth Hunter stand apart from the rest of White's major characters in that their involvement with guilt is an essential rather than an accidental aspect of their natures. Voss may not be the Great Sinner that his self-appointed role seems to demand, but he is warped and spiteful enough to attempt several acts of psychological violation and succeeds in organizing, if not actually committing, the murder of Palfreyman. Hurtle, too, has several crimes on his conscience of which he is only theoretically innocent. Elizabeth Hunter, though less warped and neurotic than Voss or Hurtle, also has a far from easy conscience. The central ethical problem that these characters present is the same, although the solutions are slightly different in each case. The following quotations indicate the problem area:

> And the cyclone: why was it given to Elizabeth Hunter to experience the eye of the storm? That too! Or are regenerative states of mind granted to the very old to ease the passage from their earthly, sensual natures into final peace and forgiveness? Of course Mother could have imagined her state of grace amongst the resting birds . . . (ES p. 73)

> And Mother: what could Mother have told of her experience on Brumby Island? She was senile by the time you might have asked. But could anything of a transcendental nature have illuminated a mind so sensual, mendacious, materialistic, superficial as Elizabeth Hunter's? (ES p. 589)

If, as the endings of the novels seem to suggest, Voss, Hurtle and Elizabeth are granted Grace in spite of the fact that, if not Great Criminals and Great Invalids, then all three are a little crooked and Voss is more than a little sick, we may be justified in asking the premises from which Patrick White's ethics develop. The obvious answer is that for Patrick White the categories of 'the ethical' and 'the spiritual' do not completely coincide. Moral flaws may be irritants or catalysts that lead to spiritual development. Ossification (and goodness can be a form of ossification) can be more spiritually damaging than perversity, since perversity carries with it the redeeming urge to 'reach the unknown'. To go beyond the normal, the reasonable, the 'decent', to be driven by a daemon or genius that expresses itself through the conquest of distance, in art or in the desire to create sensuous intoxication, is already to be exposed to a domain where justice ends and mystery begins.

This is not to say that supreme ambition, talent or social magnificence can in themselves guarantee salvation. Voss, Hurtle and Elizabeth have a more bitter and protracted contest with God than any of White's other *illuminati*. Although all three persist to the end in their chosen vocation, their final contact with God is as much in spite of as because of their external quest. Voss is only saved (if saved he is) by the intercession of his guardian saint, Laura. It is only at the very end that Hurtle Duffield finds himself a vehicle for, rather than an opponent of, the Deity he so constantly vilifies. Voss's daemon, Hurtle's gift and Mrs Hunter's élan are all, like Norbert Hare's Xanadu, their contribution to the truth—a contribution that is in part made possible by the existence of the flaws that make them morally reprehensible. But they are only contributions, not the whole truth. This is made particularly evident in the case of Elizabeth Hunter, below whose surface quest for power and admiration lies a hidden search for something else, a search that is partly the cause of her betrayals but also, finally, redeems them:

... in your own case, your idealism was too abstract, improbable, under cover of the dinner parties, the jewels, the lovers, some of them real, but more often only suspected; or else a few individuals, sensitive up to a point, had guessed at some mysterious, not religious or intellectual, some kind of spiritual aspiration, and labelled you a fraud when you couldn't confront them with, not spiritual, but material evidence. (ES p. 90)

Elizabeth Hunter, unlike Voss and Hurtle, also develops a genuine moral sense which takes her back to Kudjeri to nurse her dying husband, and she has the moral courage and honesty to face the implications of her own guilt and to feel the genuine pangs of remorse. In some ways she remains unregenerate to the very end, for nobody with a nature like hers can be totally sanctified. One of her last actions is an attempt to violate or wound her friend Lal Wyburd, and, when the attempt fails, to exact from her a dishonest avowal of love. The diabolic mask that Flora Manhood paints on her mistress is not altogether inappropriate, but it only does justice to the surface of Mrs Hunter's life and ignores the inner Grace or illumination that even Flora acknowledges in her from time to time. Whether this gift of Grace has been earned or whether it is the almost gratuitous property of nuns, idiots or some very old women (as White suggests in *The Tree of Man*) is a question that puzzles many of her visitors, in particular her children. The same puzzling question applies to all of White's central characters and is, of course, one of the knottiest problems that has faced Christianity. In White, the answer must be a combination of the two possibilities. On the one hand, Grace clearly must be a free and unconditioned gift, as the Hidden God cannot be constrained by His creatures. On the other hand, only those who have struggled stubbornly through a lifetime's pilgrimage, sometimes on the right path, often on the wrong, can reach the dangerous country where the soul is laid open to receive the Messenger. The most important distinction in White is not between 'the good' and 'the bad' but between those who have undertaken the pilgrimage and those who have stayed at home.

Good and evil are both laws of necessity that operate in the fallen world. Since it is only by passing through and experiencing inwardly all the conditions of matter that the soul can reach God, it is necessary that characters should have subjective experience of both, even though the experience of evil may only be one lapse, or the paradoxical awareness that one has innocently inflicted harm on another. Without such an experience the soul remains 'once-born'. Evil is an essential dynamic principle of spiritual growth. White does not celebrate the flower of evil for its own sake, but he is aware that without the generative seeds of evil and suffering the Rose which is his true subject could never unfold.

3
Love, Death and Rebirth

LOVE AND HATE

Love is the most celebrated and the most problematical spiritual principle in Patrick White's novels. Like the principles discussed in the last chapter, love and hate operate through the human temperament, express themselves as ethical values but ultimately have a spiritual source and a spiritual goal.

Apart from certain minor characters, such as the Johnsons in *The Aunt's Story*, the Stauffers in *Riders in the Chariot*, or the Wyburds in *The Eye of the Storm*, White does not take as his central subject a 'normal' love relationship in which habitual affection dominates and a closed circle of limited love is achieved. Where he does depict such relationships, he does so with an understanding, delicacy and sympathy that indicate that his refusal to take them as his main subject stems from a deliberate choice rather than a temperamental deficiency. He chooses to write of a more strenuous type of love, not the contentment of love achieved, but the perplexity, struggles and torments of love thwarted or distorted.

Love is a memory and a desire; it is implanted in people from the very beginning as a dim intuition, and it directs a quest through the phenomenal world towards something which lies ultimately outside that world. Some characters hear the word 'love' being used and sense in it a resonance which those around them simply do not grasp:

'I am so afraid, Norbert, we shall not love our child enough. With my health and your interests.'
'Oh, *love!*' the father replied, and laughed fit to shatter it for ever.

. . . the child learned, as far as her natural clumsiness would allow, to move softly, like a leaf, and certain words she avoided, because they were breakable. The word LOVE, for instance, brittle as glass, and far more precious. (RC p. 17)

The little girl appeared gravely to accept the attitudes adopted by her mother, but was not genuinely influenced. Unattached, she drifted through the pale waters of her mother's kindness like a little, wondering, transparent fish, in search of those depths which her instinct told her could exist. (RC p. 23)

Love flows from its original source into the created world, and as it does so, it finds its way impeded by the grossness of matter. It cannot express itself, is rejected, or is transformed into lust, jealousy, possessiveness or even hatred. The river runs into a muddy estuary and its course is turned aside, grows sluggish, meanders, loses itself in the mud, or becomes tainted and contaminated. White's novels are chronicles of the impediments that pervert the original instinct in man to love. All his writing endorses Socrates' observation in Plato's *Symposium*, that love is typified by lack, not by possession, by longing, not by fulfilment.

In *The Aunt's Story*, Theodora's capacity for affection is constantly frustrated, either because the objects of love are taken from her, like her father, Meroë, or the Man who was Given his Dinner, or else, as with Violet Adams, Frank Parrott or Huntly Clarkson, because they are emotionally inadequate to receive her love.

Stan and Amy Parker show a more complicated and paradoxical aspect of frustrated love. They both have the instinct to love but this instinct is directed to different ends. Stan loves God through nature, while Amy must find her love personalized in those around her. Their love is not mutually supporting, their different needs set up a tension and undermine each other. Her need to express love through the body is frustrated by Stan's ability to fulfil himself in nature and drives her to adultery which destroys Stan's faith in the goodness of God. We also see in the case of Amy Parker how love can be misunderstood and transformed into possessiveness or lust.

Voss's twisted and neurotic nature makes it impossible for him to open himself to the love for which he longs. Almost to the very end he resists the needs of his emotions. He senses that if he opens his stubborn soul to the earthly love that Laura, Palfreyman and Judd represent and offer, it will make him vulnerable to divine love, which would undermine his own pretensions to divinity.

All four Riders experience forms of thwarted or frustrated love. Mary Hare and Alf Dubbo both have their capacity to love human beings crushed in their childhood. Mary Hare hates humanity because of the way it reacts to her misshapen form and unusual temperament, while Alf discovers through experience that when white people offer him love or affection it always ends in lust or betrayal. They can both love God in nature, or in those parts of the Bible which show Him in non-human forms, but cannot cope with the implications of the Gospels in which Love is given a human face. Himmelfarb and Ruth Godbold, on the other hand, never lose their light of loving kindness for humanity but find no channel through which to express it; their desire to serve, atone and testify is not acceptable to others. Himmelfarb is not needed by the Chosen People, and Ruth only torments those she wishes to save.

Waldo Brown, like Voss, is locked up in the icy citadel of the ego, holding love at arm's length. Like Voss, he desperately longs for love, and like Voss he lashes out at those who might give it to him. Unlike Voss, however, the redemptive power never breaks through his defences, and he dies of his own hatred. This is the most detailed and explicit account White has written of how the potential for love can be transformed into its lethal opposite number. Arthur, on the other hand, is like Ruth and Himmelfarb, a generator of love which the grossness of the clay from which he is created prevents him expressing. His unprepossessing exterior and lumbering mind alienate many of those who should be the recipients of his gift.

Hurtle Duffield is one of the most bedevilled of all White's characters by the problematical nature of love. From his early sense of guilt about preferring Mrs Courtney to his real mother, through to his admission in old age that he has never been able to love Rhoda, his life is spent in cycles of emotional need, emotional inadequacy, betrayal and counter-betrayal. He constantly fails people in love, but his guilt is tempered by the fact that those he has failed have, in turn, held false attitudes towards him. The ponce and the prostitute are symbols for most of the relationships in the book; Hurtle feeds off others, while they use him to fulfil something in their lives of which he is only a partial expression. Love is at its most convoluted and distorted in this and the following novel.

Elizabeth Hunter, in *The Eye of the Storm*, has the word 'love' constantly in her mind or on her lips. Sometimes this is the expression of petulant senile infantilism:

'I hate Badgery.'

'I hate all those other women.' Mrs Hunter had mustered her complete stubbornness this morning. 'It's only you I love, Sister de Santis.' She directed at the nurse that milky stare which at times still seemed to unshutter glimpses of a terrifying mineral blue. (ES p. 10)

Sometimes it may appear in a sardonic if revealing epigram:

'The worst thing about love between human beings,' the voice was directed at her from the bed, 'when you're prepared to love them they don't want it; when they do, it is you who can't bear the idea.' (ES p. 11)

Sometimes it is expressed in a pregnant anecdote, like that of the murdered lovebird (ES pp. 59–61) or of Kate Nutley's murdered sister (ES p. 24). It is only too evident in Elizabeth Hunter's case that 'love' is not always a positive word. It can mask frigidity and emotional blackmail, lust for power or a cannibalistic desire to devour the lives of others. As mentioned in the last chapter, one of Mrs Hunter's last acts, masquerading in the guise of love, is an attempt to make a conquest of the intransigently honest Lal Wyburd, an attempt that shows no matter'how 'hallowed' part of Elizabeth's nature may be, the old greedy serpent is still alive and hungry:

'Will you kiss me, Lal?' she asked.

Mrs Hunter was raising her blind head on the end of its ringed neck: the effect was ancient and reptilian. Lal Wyburd felt herself contained in what might have been an envelope of vapour, or sentimental pity, inside which, again, her mind was reared in horror, not for the decayed humanity she had at her mercy, but beyond the mask, still the legend of Elizabeth Hunter's beauty.

And now here below Mrs Hunter's lips were probing trembling around at nothing.

Quickly Mrs Wyburd stooped: she kissed the air just short of the older woman's face.

Elizabeth Hunter must have heard it. She sank back on her pillows looking fairly well satisfied.

'Love me!' she murmured, scarcely for her caller.

It might have been another conquest, not so much of an individual as of the abstract: in any case, she would chalk it up along with the others. (ES p. 536)

So White, through much of his writing, is recording the difficulties or perversities of love, rather than its fulfilment. We must now examine how the cycle of descent and return applies in the case of this particular principle.

Love of God must first be learned and expressed through love of the incarnation. 'Pure' love of God cannot come into being by denying the flesh, as Kierkegaard did, but by union with it. The carnal embrace, of which the most obvious form is the sexual union, is a spiritual necessity. White is not 'Lawrentian' in his attitude towards carnality; his views are closer to those of Plato, with certain important exceptions that shall be mentioned. But compassion, as Voss observes, is a grace of some sensual origin (V p. 227), and the union with the flesh is a necessary step towards union with God. Many mystics have expressed the Divine union in sexual terms, and although they tend to rationalize this usage as being merely metaphorical, one senses that there is indeed a close organic link between carnality and spirituality. The full implications of this remark will be discussed in Chapter Six.

The soul must begin its pilgrimage by embracing the flesh. This is the lesson that the Young Man in *The Ham Funeral* must learn: only by going down to the sweaty embrace of Alma Lusty can he find his true role. Elyot Standish learns to accept the link between himself and the queazy drunk who was run over. Laura Trevelyan must embrace the body of her maid and Himmelfarb must accept the intimacy of the warm, sickly body of Israel the dyer.

On the human plane, love for God is expressed through love of His incarnation. Love must be roused by, and directed towards, a particular individual. In all of White's novels, characters find their God in a human form. Theodora in the figment of Holstius, Amy in Stan, Harry and Frank in Voss, Mrs Godbold and Mary Hare in Himmelfarb, and Mrs Poulter in Arthur Brown. This is particularly true of the women in White's novels; God is too vast to be embraced directly, and a local habitation must be found for Him. This accounts for the merging of the individual with the figure of Christ in *Voss* and *Riders in the Chariot*, but it is also true in the books where Christianity is not explicitly present.

The driving force of *The Vivisector* is the displacement of spiritual need into sexuality. All the women in the book make demands on Hurtle which begin as erotic, but eventually reveal a hidden factor that carries them into another dimension. Mrs Courtney looks through, rather than at, the men in her life. She is hunting for something which is still couched in purely sentimental or sexual terms, something that is not yet understood as spiritual. This impulse drives her, after her marriage has dried up, to make incestuous movements in Hurtle's direction, and finally leads her to marry the young Julian Boileau. This is how Mrs Courtney herself views it:

'Nor do I think girls grow up into anything very different from what they were. They're still blundering about after they've promised to honour and obey. Oh, I don't mean they're dishonest—not all of them—but they're still quivering and preparing to discover something they haven't experienced yet.' (Viv p. 169)

With Nance Lightfoot, the unacknowledged factor behind the sexual drive becomes slightly more explicit, although her limited temperament makes her express her longings in terms of banal romance. She 'falls in love' with Hurtle and blames his egocentricity when he fails to fulfil her daydreams. It emerges, however, that she has fallen in love not with, but through, Hurtle, using him as the embodiment of a mythical man-figure who, in turn, relates to her inchoate longing for spiritual experience. Nance usually takes a purely practical, matter-of-fact attitude towards her profession, but lets slip towards the end a revealing confession:

'It's funny,' she said, 'you go on the job and know more or less what you'll get. It's what you never find that keeps you at it.' (Viv p. 236)

Later, she elaborates the adolescent source of her erotico-religious quest, and also makes it quite plain to Hurtle that he has been a stand-in for something else:

'That night in Rushcutters bloody Park when I got caught up with Duffield it was that old digger's coat you was wearun I got a sight of it it had the green look of old pennies as I'd always imagined and nothun you did or said would'uv thrown me off though it wasn't hairy like I'd always imagined the overcoat would be.' (Viv p. 257)

'This man I never me I hoped could'uv taught me somethun I mightn't'uv otherwise understood. Not about sex. Well, about sex as well. I used to stick me fist in me mouth and bite it and rub me arms on the dry seaweed till they looked like they had a rash. Sometimes the birds flew so low I could feel the noise of their wings and got the idea my head might be split open and would swallow up one of those white birds then when the wound had closed I would see things as they're supposed to be . . . There was a girl I knew her name was Eileen Gilchrist Sister Scolastica they called her after she'd been shaved. I often wonder if she found what she was lookun for when she went whoorun after all those bally saints.' (Viv pp. 255–6)

In the case of Hero Pavloussi, we see even more clearly the connection, but now also the tension, between sexual and spiritual love. She has a deep longing for an absolute of goodness and purity, which she embodies in the form of her husband. When he rejects her because of her passionate nature, she feels that she has been rejected by, and is unworthy of, God, and converts her innocent 'blasphemy' into a deliberate programme of self-destruction, aimed as much at God as at herself. As her self-inflicted contamination increases, so does her desire for a redemptive miracle. When she reaches Perialos, however, she finds not the sanctity she has hoped for, but only more concupiscence and a derisive pile of dung. Unlike Hurtle she cannot see that these, as much as the mythical purity for which she longs, may be aspects of God.

In Hero's case sexuality and spirituality have got out of phase, which suggests that the connection between them, though profound, is not absolute. This is made even more evident in the case of Elizabeth Hunter who, in spite of all her surface deviousness, understands better than any of White's other women characters the wellsprings of her own nature. She makes manifest that which was latent in the other novels, showing clearly the metaphysical goal of the apparently carnal quest:

'... Poor Lilian—my other Nutley! She hadn't begun to learn that love is not a matter of lovers—even the least murderous one. So she had to die.' (ES pp. 169–70)

'... Later, and last of all, I longed to possess people who would obey me—and love me of course. Can you understand all this?'

'Whatever they tell you, I loved my husband. My children wouldn't allow me to love them.' The stole had dragged so far behind, it was lost to her by catching on what must have been an invisible splinter.

'Oh, I know I am not selfless enough!' When she turned she was burning with a blue, inward rage; but quickly quenched it, and drew up a stool at this girl's feet. 'There is this other love, I know. Haven't I been shown? And I still can't reach it. But I shall! I shall!' (ES p. 162)

... oh yes bestiality is familiar didn't you choose to rut with that that politician Athol Thingummy you know it down to the last bristle the final spurt of lust and renounce men anyway for tonight.

Now surely, at the end of your life, you can expect to be shown the inconceivable something you have always, it seems, been looking for. (ES p. 544)

There is, in fact, a profound metaphysical and temperamental ambivalence running through White's novels. The necessity of embracing the body is coupled, from his earliest books, with a deep aversion to it. We feel this in the Young Man and Elyot Standish as much as we do in Voss, the later Hurtle Duffield and Mrs Hunter. Even while the fleshly embrace is celebrated, it is shunned. The embrace is often an act of will as much as of inclination, and the end of the cycle is the rejection of the flesh for the sake of a purely spiritual union.

Love of the body and of the individual is a necessary but not a sufficient condition for true spiritual love, and those who are governed too completely by their carnal impulses destroy, rather than fulfil, the destiny which these impulses should subserve. This is most obvious in the case of Hero Pavloussi, but it is also seen in

Catherine Standish, Amy Parker and many of the women in the plays
and short stories.

The temperamental and metaphysical ambivalence in regard to the
flesh is expressed through the emphasis which White places on those
who deviate from the normal standards of human beauty. Many of his
characters are deformed or extremely ugly. He emphasizes constantly
the hare-lip, the hump, the slobbering mouth, the monstrous nose,
the stumpy limbs or repulsive hairiness of his characters. He seems to
be reversing Plato's emphasis on physical perfection and suggests instead that beauty in the conventional sense is an aberration from,
rather than an expression of, the true nature of life. The destiny of
man in the fallen world is its imperfection, and it is only by embracing the flesh in its more imperfect forms that one can truly love
the destiny that God has prescribed. Like success, beauty is an end in
itself; ugliness, like failure, points to a higher end. By the difficult act
of accepting the connection between the self and the repulsive, as
Laura Trevelyan does with Rose Portion and Himmelfarb does with
Mary Hare, one achieves a higher and therefore more rewarding
mode of love.

Love for the individual, with the promise of individual happiness
that accompanies it, must be sacrificed, in the last stage of the cycle,
for love of something impersonal that exists on a higher plane. In
Happy Valley, Oliver Halliday struggles between his desire for personal happiness with Alys Browne and his awareness of his duty
towards a larger pattern. Alys and Oliver quicken personal love in
each other, but this love must finally be absorbed into 'the pattern'.
Oliver turns once more to the claims of duty made by his family and
'the sick world', while Alys resolves her problem in almost Buddhist
terms, finding contentment through contemplation of the still pool of
life. In *The Living and the Dead*, Eden encounters the same problem in
her relationship with Joe Barnett and comes to the same conclusion:

> Out of this world you could feel a purpose forming. Just as she had seen,
> after refusing, a purpose that formed behind his eyes. It was not a malicious
> desire to annihilate that cancelled the personal relationship, that bound the
> earth in its harder seasons. The stripping of the bough was a sacrifice of detail
> to some ultimate and superior design. To dictate this to the heart, impress it
> on the mind, is necessary, she felt. Bark was cool on her forehead. I have to
> accept, to believe this, she said, because it is the only way, I must blot out all
> memory of touch, or the more intimate moments of silence. (LD p. 309)

We find this necessary sacrifice of detail for the sake of a larger
design in all White's novels. Love for the particular must ultimately be

renounced or sacrificed for love of the All. This act of self-sacrifice is sometimes reluctant, sometimes willingly accepted, but it must always be effected and endorsed, or the individual will die, as he has lived, imprisoned in the particular. Stan Parker, for instance, learns painfully that he must have everything taken from him—the natural world that he loves, his farm and even his life. By being prepared to let go rather than to cling, as does his wife, he ends by having everything restored to him on a higher plane. He loses his own small corner of nature but is granted possession, through his dying vision of cosmic unity, of all Nature.

The concept of 'sacrifice' is developed further in *Voss*, where there is a constant dialectic between the pagan sacrifice to the Self that Voss expects of his followers and the Christian ideal of self-sacrifice practised by Laura. Even the self-immolation which Voss realizes may be in store for him in the desert is not sacrifice of the self but sacrifice to the self. Laura counters this pagan ideal with acts of self-renunciation based on humility rather than pride. Her sacrifice is a subdued and unspectacular one, amounting to no less than rejection of all claims to personal love and happiness. It culminates in her attempt to give up her child Mercy as a token of her willingness to suffer for the sake of Voss's soul. That this attempt fails is not relevant to the intention; failure is its own form of success.

This drive for self-renunciation on Laura's part marks her off from most heroines of fiction, and suggests affinities instead with such figures as Beatrice of *The Divine Comedy* or the Gretchen who intercedes for Faust at the end of Goethe's play. Laura has a tendency, which grows throughout the book, to express her feelings for Voss not in tender, personal, but in generic, almost harsh or scornful terms. Even during the early stages of personal love for Voss, she never mitigated or excused his faults, and as she undergoes her *imitatio Christi* her attitude towards him seems almost entirely devoid of particular reference. She speaks not as a loving wife but as an interceding saint:

'Except,' she said, distorting her mouth with an irony which intensified the compassion that she felt, and now was compelled to express, 'except that man is so shoddy, so contemptible, greedy, jealous, stubborn, ignorant. Who will love him when I am gone? I only pray that God will.' (V p. 411)

This attitude prevails in the 'coda' of the novel. In later life, Laura has a detached and nun-like devotion which seems directed not at Voss's memory in particular but at humanity in general. This nun-

like withdrawal is not a temperamental deficiency but a deliberate act
of personal sacrifice:

> The vows were rigorous that she imposed upon herself, to the exclusion of all
> personal life, certainly of introspection, however great her longing for those
> delights of hell. The gaunt man, her husband, would not tempt her in. (V p.
> 430)

The cycle of love moves from an initial love of the incarnation, love
of the particular and of the flesh, even in its most imperfect forms,
through a deepening spiritual awareness born of this love, to a final
surrender of personal love for the sake of union with a higher and less
personal Love. This higher Love is expressed to the end in sensuous
or mythical terms but points beyond the novels to a final union of the
soul with God. These preliminary remarks, like many others of Part
One, will be extended and amplified in Parts Two and Three.

LIFE, DEATH AND REBIRTH

Life and death twine around each other in Patrick White's novels. The
rose and the rock, flesh and bone, skeleton and spawn constantly
counterpoint and complete one another. The inevitability of physical
death forces itself on the minds of the living, and is often the
touchstone of their spiritual resources. The action of the books swings
between the poles of plenitude and vacancy, burgeoning with
vegetable life or shrivelling to dust and ashes: '"You cannot reconcile
life and death. For this reason, Theodora Goodman, you must
accept."'; 'Out of the rusted tin welled the brown circles of perpetual
water, stirring with great gentleness the eternal complement of
skeleton and spawn.'

Voss, for example, clearly shows the constant dialectic between
these opposite principles. On the one hand there are all the affirmations of life: roses, pregnancy, the beauty of the land under the
transforming power of light, the glowing textures of parties, picnics
and dances which are almost magic rites, and the presence of children
in the closing pages. Balancing these, however, are the *mementi mori*:
images of rock and bone, grey ash and cinders, skulls, sepulchres,
cemeteries, gothic vaults, saints on slabs, rotting flesh and corpses. As
the characters wind deeper into their suffering, this sepulchral at-
mosphere deepens. The *mementi mori* of European Catholicism and
their gothic resonances blend with the death cults of the desert—the
burial platforms, the spiritistic eschatology and the aboriginal
Dreamtime—to evoke a new and extremely powerful Australian

death mystery. We feel the semi-comic, semi-macabre influence of mediaeval representations of Death in the following passage:

As for Mrs Bonner, she did suffer a great deal, less in sorrow for her dead servant, than from the presence, the very weight of Death, for while she had been struggling up the crumbly slope, recalling the different illnesses that had carried off her relatives and friends, He had mounted pick-aback, and there He rode, regardless of a lady's feelings. (V p. 250)

The blending of the two streams of mythology is suggested by Boyle of Jildra:

'Why, anyone who is disposed can celebrate a high old Mass, I do promise, with the skull of a blackfeller and his own blood, in Central Australia.' (V p. 180)

Life and death are both principles that rule the incarnate condition, so acceptance of life must mean acceptance of death. It is the emotionally and spiritually depleted characters, like Waldo Brown, who are afraid of death. The culminating vision of which we have spoken in the preceding chapters, in which 'man returns to God', often occurs at or near the moment of death. Death tests and crowns the quality of life. In the words of Simone Weil:

. . . I never allowed myself to think of a future state, but I always believed that the instant of death is the centre and object of life. I used to think that, for those who live as they should, it is the instant when for an infinitesimal fraction of time, pure truth, naked, certain and eternal enters the soul.[9]

Elizabeth Hunter has the courage to acknowledge both the difficulty and the importance of the moment of death:

She hadn't been praying for you, surely? For that thing your soul; or an easy death. Extraordinary the number of people who insist that death must be painless and easy when it ought to be the highest, the most difficult peak of all: that is its whole point. (ES p. 190)

This does not mean that White's metaphysic is essentially death-oriented. Those who experience the final vision are not those who have denied life, but those who have lived out life at its deepest and most meaningful level. Those for whom death is no more than the moment of physical disintegration, the last of the chemical changes, are those who have only experienced the semblance of life and have not really lived at all.

The death of the individual is transcended by two modes of continuity. On the one hand, there is the continuity and renewal of life on
the organic level; almost all the novels have a coda suggesting the fact
that a new cycle will begin as the old exhausts itself. The doctor who
attends the dying Mrs O'Dowd in *The Tree of Man* has just been
delivering a baby, while the novel as a whole ends, not with the death
of Stan, but with the assertion of new life in his grandson, who is
linked with the eternal trees, and is going to write a poem about the
Whole of Life. Children crowd into the closing pages of the novels as
the cycle is completed and death overtakes the former generation.
Mrs Godbold, at the end of *Riders in the Chariot*, affirms her role as the
principle of organic renewal and her obedience to God's first com-
mandment, which was: 'Be fruitful and multiply'.

So her arrows would continue to be aimed at the forms of darkness, and she
herself was, in fact, the infinite quiver.
   'Multiplication!' Mrs Godbold loudly declared . . . (RC p. 549)

This continuity, this passing on of the torch, is a spiritual as well as
a biological fact. The sparks of wisdom or intuition of the aged or
dying are sensed by the young and become the starting point for a new
spiritual quest. Theodora Goodman is given early glimpses of
something larger by Father and the Man who was Given his Dinner,
and, in turn, implants seeds of awareness in Lou and Zack. Holstius
remarks: '"Faces inherit features. Thought and experience are
bequeathed."' (AS p. 299). Laura Trevelyan is last seen activating dormant intuitions in the young and making artists aware of their true
vocation, while Hurtle Duffield passes his creative intuition on to
Kathy Volkov. At the end of *The Eye of the Storm*, Mary de Santis is
preparing to pass on the wisdom, the suffering and the illumination
that she has acquired during the course of her relationship with
Elizabeth Hunter to the young crippled girl Irene who, by Grace, may
be softened or redeemed by contact with this inherited wisdom.

The death of the individual is also transcended by hints of a continued life on a higher plane. White seldom does more than hint at
what may happen after death, although in certain places he does
follow the soul a few steps. White limits himself on the subject of life
after death in the same way that Arthur Brown does:

Till in the centre of their mandala he danced the passion of all their lives,
the blood running out of the backs of his hands, water out of the hole in his
ribs . . .
   And then, when he had been spewed up, spat out, with the breeze stripping

him down to the saturated skin, and the fit almost withdrawn from him, he added the little quivering footnote on forgiveness. (SM p. 267)

At times there is a definite question-mark hanging over the moment of death, and the quivering footnote on forgiveness is very muted:

> As for the head-thing, it knocked against a few stones, and lay like any melon. How much was left of the man it no longer represented? His dreams fled into the air, his blood ran out upon the dry earth, which drank it up immediately. Whether dreams breed, or the earth responds to a pint of blood, the instant of death does not tell. (V p. 419)

The question is posed and never answered directly, but a numinous cloud of directional hints and clues envelops the deaths of Patrick White's central characters and suggests irresistibly that for those who have found Grace, or have had Grace forced upon them, the moment of death is a *rite de passage* into endless life. In *Voss*, the blend of Christian and aboriginal beliefs extends to eschatology. The first stage in the departure from the body is thought of in purely spiritistic terms. Souls fly out of bodies like birds, or stay to haunt certain localities where their owners had died. In the case of Voss himself, the soul actually takes up temporary residence, it is suggested, in the body of Jackie, and uses him as a medium (as later, in less animistic forms, it uses Laura). Frank Le Mesurier's poem 'Conclusions' suggests the two-stage progression of the soul after death, the first stage being native, the second being Christian:

> O God, my God, I pray that you will take my spirit out of this my body's remains, and after you have scattered it, grant that it shall be everywhere, and in the rocks, and in the empty water-holes, and in true love of all men, and in you, O God, at last. (V pp. 316–17)

So far we have been discussing the question of physical death, but as the title of *The Living and the Dead* suggests, White is also concerned, particularly in his early novels, with the problem of emotional and spiritual death. This is, of course, the central theme of *The Living and the Dead*, in which there is wholesale 'death', seen in terms of listlessness, flaccidity, fear, indifference and apathy. After this novel—perhaps White had resolved certain temperamental or artistic problems of his own—this is never again the central subject of his books. Whatever problems his later characters have, they possess an inner vitality and life which makes them refreshingly free from that spiritual torpor that afflicts Elyot Standish. Even so, there are certain processes in this early book, related to the theme of death and rebirth, which are relevant to the later novels.

In this book a twin spiral can be seen, in which processes of degeneration and regeneration are locked together in a vortex, highlighting each other by contrast and relief. Catherine Standish, in spite of her surface liveliness, is caught in a self-perpetuating downward spiral. Every moment in life, every vignette in the novel, is a crossroad, a challenge presented by the archetypal experiences of life through which everybody must pass. At each crossroad, because of her emotional inadequacy, she takes the wrong turn. She trivializes each important experience as it occurs. She cannot rise to the challenge of being teacher, lover, wife or mother; she cannot cope with pregnancy or jealousy, with the challenge of the mind or the problem of old age. She develops a habitually evasive mode of response which is not condemned ethically, but is shown destroying her almost as organically as the cancer from which she dies. She never enters into fruitful dialogue with the potentially creative principles of existence and ends in a state of disintegration.

In her son we see both the downward spiral and also the upward movement of regeneration. By birth he is endowed with only limited emotional resources; he is inward, cold, self-enclosed and has little vital energy. He does, however, possess a few sparks of reality—an impulse to love, an awareness of beauty and a capacity to respond to simple goodness in others. These sparks are almost extinguished during his formative years by his inability to find anyone with whom he can have a meaningful relationship. From his early anxiety dreams, his fears of the War and his sense of rejection, up to his affair with Hildegaard and his sojourn at Cambridge, he is surrounded by false attitudes, which his own sluggish resources are too weak to overcome. The irony of his situation is that he needs to enter into relationships if his latent capacity is to be nurtured, but if he relates to those around him on their terms he will falsify himself and violate his own integrity and discernment. (This is also the paradox that plagues much of Theodora Goodman's life in Part One of *The Aunt's Story*.) Elyot enters a state of living death, entrenched in arid academicism and sterile, rational sexuality, which persists for ten years.

The second half of the novel shows a slow reversal of this process. The memory of the few positive moments in his childhood is activated by contact with Joe Barnett, and by his awareness of the love between Eden and Joe. Just as all the events of the first section had pushed him downward, so the events of the latter part help him to rebirth. Images of the egg begin to appear towards the end of the book as Elyot stirs in his shell. Even the deaths of his mother, Joe and the queasy drunk, and the departure of Eden for Spain, contribute to his awakening. The last step in the process is the experience of recapitulation from which the novel as a whole emanates. The technique White uses is not just the literary device of the 'flashback'. It is an organic part of Elyot's experience, serving a psychotherapeutic function, allowing him to probe the springs of his own nature, bring the hidden traumas to consciousness, and see in its totality the pattern that has emerged from his life.

Elyot appears, at the beginning of the book, as the deadest of the dead. This appearance is deceptive; his rebirth has not been a steady progression but a series of upward movements followed by troughs, relapses into states of exhaustion and inertia. As the book opens, we find him in the last and deepest of these troughs before the breakthrough. Such a period of spiritual or emotional depletion seems to be necessary to the regenerative process. In this fallow condition, the vital forces of the unconscious are active; as the last remnants of the old pattern are sloughed off, in a moment of despair and detachment, a new one rises up to assert itself. This necessary black night of the soul occurs to almost all of White's major characters, and is summed up in Hurtle Duffield's pitch black painting that he is forced to execute before his final affirmations.

The twin spirals of degeneration and regeneration, the movements towards collapse or rebirth, are seen in all the later novels. In *The Solid Mandala*, Waldo, after a lifetime of false existential choices, sinks down into a death that is more than just physical, while Arthur completes his upward climb by being reborn (once more after a black night of despair) through Mrs Poulter.

In *The Vivisector*, Hurtle lives out his life through a series of 'deaths' which are similar in some ways to those of Waldo, but each of which is followed by a rebirth onto a higher plane. Hurtle himself becomes aware of this cycle after his conversation with Mothersole:

His teeth grated as he regurgitated the nonsense he had talked while in the throes of rebirth; Hero's death; his own; that of his paintings ... He remembered another occasion when he had risen from the dead, by seminal dew and the threats of moonlight, in conversation, repulsive, painful but necessary, with the grocer Cutbush, and now was born again by grace of Mothersole's warm middle-class womb. (Viv p. 421)

The indissoluble link between the organic and the spiritual and between death and rebirth are expressed in Hurtle's last painting of Hero, with its hope for a resurrection:

... the cancer glowed inside the monstrance of Hero's womb as the wooden saints of Perialos raised her up ...
How could his unborn child fail to stir amongst these miracles of the risen dead? (Viv p. 422)

The image of the vortex that has been used in the preceding discussion appears most overtly in *The Eye of the Storm*. In this novel, there is a complicated overlaying of rising and falling rhythms, all revolving around the dying Mrs Hunter who is herself sucked into a private maelstrom of memory and guilt but is, through the very velocity of the emotional cyclone, pitched past pitch of grief to the point where anguish ends and illumination begins. But, as in *The Living and the Dead*, it is on the son, not on the mother, that the theme of rebirth is concentrated. Sir Basil Hunter's impoverishment is more than financial, and behind the apparently mercenary motives for his return to Australia lies a quest for artistic and personal rebirth which involves a confrontation with his mother and with the memory of his father, the union with his sister, his return to Kudjeri, and the experiment in living theatre—his 'suicide play'—that awaits him in London. The driving force behind all of these is his desire to act, or, rather, to achieve Lear, which is a part that cannot, he believes, be played by an actor but only by a whole human being. Basil Hunter is not unaware of the farcical elements in his own nature and in his quest for rebirth, but behind the vaudeville and slapstick of the following dream sequences lies the same artistic and personal imperative that structured *The Living and the Dead* and *The Ham Funeral*:

The room did become yours as far as sleep could persuade a vast black chamber in which naked tumblers were playing a scene from birth to death it was the only scene in the play Mitty explaining for that reason fairly elastic somebody pulls your frightened prick to remind you the tumblers have formed a womb out of their stacked bodies through which you were expected to crawl under the encrustations of swallows'-nests out between the mare's legs whether Mitty approved of her Primordial Baby's interpretation you couldn't tell nor look to see whether Mother (ES p. 143)

... the young trolls are lining up together with their liquescent warlocks to build this tunnel thing bet it wasn't improvised ENTER A BEARDLESS KING ... LILAC KING opens her legs go on Bas on all fours natch it's the womb stint you've got to expect in living theatre well it happens doesn't it they pull you through beneath the lilac pubics ... at least you are born at last MITTY blacktights JACKA *HE is born our King of Kings* (crack) forward Basssll *well folks here I am this is my real role your fool* . . . (ES pp. 593–4)

The young crypto-artist Elyot Standish in 1940 and the world-famous knight actor of 1973 are, in spite of the thirty-three years between them, wrestling with the same artistic and spiritual problems, and the conclusion of Basil's section of *The Eye of the Storm* is as open-ended as the conclusions of *The Living and the Dead* and *The Ham Funeral*. Sir Basil Hunter is last seen taking a leap into the dark of an unborn future, heading back to London for his 'suicide play' and beyond that to peaks not yet attained. It is a confident assertion of the endless possibilities of artistic revitalization and renewal.

4

The Prison and the Flood

FORM AND CHAOS

The principles to be discussed in this chapter are more abstract than those of the preceding ones but nevertheless have vital emotional, ethical and spiritual meaning for the individual. Human life maintains a precarious foothold between the worlds of form and flux, just as the Hôtel du Midi in *The Aunt's Story* is perched perilously between the cactus garden and the ocean. These two conditions are largely suggested through imagery and will be discussed more fully in Part Three.

Both form and chaos can be potent for either destruction or salvation according to the way they are encountered by the individual. Form can be experienced either as a state of bondage and imprisonment or as an expression of the indissoluble unity of the individual with the totality; Arthur Brown discovers the latter aspect of form in an encyclopaedia definition of the mandala:

> *The mandala is a symbol of totality. It is believed to be the 'dwelling of the god'. Its protective circle is a pattern of order super-imposed on—psychic—chaos* . . . (SM p. 238)

Flux can either be feared as the destructive element—the flood—or else embraced as the endlessness of pure Being; Mrs Hunter discovers it in the latter aspect at the moment of death:

> . . . let us rather—enfold.
> Till I am no longer filling the void with mock substance: myself is this endlessness. (ES p. 551)

It is necessary for the soul to descend into the world of forms in order to complete and fulfil itself, but in doing so it finds itself imprisoned. The prison can be as intimate as the body itself, as can be seen in these quotations from *The Tree of Man*:

His body was hardening into the sculptural shape of muscular bodies. And for the casual speculator there was no obvious sign that his soul too might not harden in the end into the neat, self-contained shape it is desirable souls should take. (TM p. 38)

The gathering darkness and the nets of blackberries pressed her thin soul into greater confinement, and the child inside her protested, perhaps sensing some future frustration, already in the prison of her bones. (TM p. 60)

He knew that where his cart had stopped, he would stop. There was nothing to be done. He would make the best of this cell in which he had been locked. (TM p. 7)

She would have dragged him back if she could, to share her further sentence, which she could not contemplate for that moment, except in terms of solitary confinement. (TM p. 497)

Form is necessary to matter, to shape and give security to the soul, which is fearful of too much reality. But the soul may be stunted if it lives only a narrow and enclosed life, never realizing that there is something larger into which it could be released. The 'led life' in houses, the habitual patterns of family and social behaviour and the structuring of identity around the ego give form and security at the expense of illumination.

On the other hand, a life which is rooted, which has an organic form, derived from growing in one spot, does possess a spiritual value, which those who have given themselves over to the quest for 'freedom' lose. This is one of the central themes of *The Tree of Man*, the action of which is pivoted around the contrast between the rooted life, symbolized by the tree and the rose, and the 'free' life of the city dwellers. White is essentially a quietist, and those who have uprooted themselves and given themselves over to pure 'doing' eventually wither away. In *Riders in the Chariot*, for instance, he gives this picture of a society given over to the dance of suburban futility:

. . . it was not unusual for people to run outside and jump into their cars . . . They would drive and look for something to look at. Until motion became an expression of truth, the only permanence . . . So the owners of the homes drove. They drove around. (RC p. 546)

Although the cell of the body and of the led life must be transcended, it is not necessary, or even desirable, to uproot oneself completely. Flux, expressed in images of water, fire and wind, is all around and exists also in the soul. One has only to open one's eyes.

Flux has two natures, and how it is regarded is determined by the spiritual capacity of the character. On the one hand, it is primordial chaos, the destroyer of identity and eroder of form, the enemy of personal security and happiness. It is in this aspect that it predominates in *The Living and the Dead*. On the other hand, it is the numinous world of pure Being, from which the phenomenal world emanates. This is the sense in which it is found in *The Aunt's Story*:

> 'Through eternity,' added Theodora Goodman.
> 'Alas,' sighed Sokolnikov.
> But Theodora did not reject the word. It flowed, violet, and black, and momentarily oyster-bellied through the evening landscape, fingering the faces of the houses. Soon the sea would merge with the houses, and the almost empty asphalt promenade, and the dissolving lavender hills behind the town. So that there was no break in the continuity of being. The landscape was a state of interminable being, hope and despair devouring and disgorging endlessly, and the faces, whether Katina Pavlou, or Sokolnikov, or Mrs Rapallo, or Wetherby, only slightly different aspects of the same state. (AS p. 188)

As was said above, the aspect that prevails depends largely on the resources of the character involved. Amy Parker's predominant emotion at the time of the flood is insecurity, but Stan, though by now adhering to the fixed life, responds to something deeper in it, linked with memories of his early wanderings, his reading of an old copy of Shakespeare (damaged in a flood) and his mother's death. He is also aware of the magic and the mystery of fire, remaining grave and thoughtful, or else blazing up with inner poetry, while other men are laughing and joking. Again, in *The Solid Mandala*, Waldo Brown's section is filled with visions of flood, flux and chaos. Waldo is constantly menaced by waves of grass or storm-clouds, but Arthur's section is almost entirely free of these images of the destructive element.

The most complete study of the relationship between the individual and the world of Being is found in *The Aunt's Story*. The numinous world may well have ontological priority over the phenomenal world, but this is not to say that those who are aware of it, necessary as their glimpses may be, wish to lose themselves completely in it. The soul may be homesick for eternity, but it is even more homesick, at least until the very end, for the world of touching forms. Theodora Goodman is not a philosopher, but through experience, instinct and madness she is gifted or cursed with a kind of reluctant platonism. Though hungry for reality, she remains profoundly sceptical that this quality can be ascribed to the natural world:

> Why then, said Theodora Goodman, is this world which is so tangible in appearance so difficult to hold?

Because she herself, in contradiction to the confidence of Mrs Johnson's photograph, could not answer for the substance of the marble clock. She went nervously and touched the clock. Her hands slid over the surface, not of objects, but of appearances. (AS p. 287)

These doubts about the reality of substance culminate in a vision of complete dissolution of appearances shortly before Holstius visits her:

Seen from the solitude of the house the process of disintegration that was taking place at the foot of the mountains should have been frightening and tragic, but jt was not. The shapes of disintegrating light protested less than the illusions of solidity with which men surround themselves. Theodora now remembered with distaste the ugly and unnatural face of the Johnsons' orange marble clock. Because the death rattle of time is far more acute, and painful, and prolonged, when its impermanence is disguised as permanence. (AS p. 290)

From the metaphysical point of view such a vision may be the 'truth' but from a psychological point of view (as we shall see in a later chapter) it is a sickness of which Theodora must be cured. Like all mental pathology it is not a comfortable condition to be in. Theodora doubts the solidity of the world, the permanence of identity, the reality of the touch of hands and temporal continuity but yearns for them. The mysticism of objects in this book is generated by her deep nostalgia for a world of form which she can no longer trust.

The numinous world drifts around man, giving him glimpses of a higher reality, a greater ecstasy and more agonizing sickness than are usual in his enclosed existence. Such moments of reality are necessary for the soul, preventing it from setting in the same mould as its imprisoning flesh. At the same time, man cannot live with this awareness all his life. The disturbing short story 'A Woman's Hand' shows vividly the traumatic consequences for those who look too deeply into the lethal mystery and do not have the temperament to sustain the voltage. White is a novelist, not a guru, and as a novelist, even a religious one, he must be in love with the things of this world. He deals in words, themselves finite forms, and through words he constructs as solidly as he can an imitation of the world of the Many. Were he to treat only his awareness of the formless world beyond matter, he could never write novels at all, but would content himself with the One Word. His characters, too, live out their lives in the world of forms, for which they are hungry and through which they are incubated. Life can only briefly be lived in pure intensity; for most of the time it moves through extension, which is its foster home.

Both form and chaos can be destructive at stage two of the spiritual cycle. Fleshly existence and the various forms through which it manifests itself can become a prison whose four-square walls can cramp or even obliterate the soul's inklings of eternity. The formless world of Being can be experienced as a lethal flood whose demonic current sweeps away security, personal happiness, sanity and life itself. Yet by the paradoxical law of antinomy that works throughout White's novels, both form and flux can also be agents of redemption. At the final moment of theophany, apotheosis or Grace, their demonic aspects are shaken off and they become interchangeable symbols for the moment of infolding. The terrifying world of Chaos is transformed into the tranquil sea of Brahman; the imprisoning cell of form reveals its transcendental aspect as the soul is incorporated into the firm geometry of the cosmic mandala. Thesis and antithesis are merged into a simultaneous symbol which will wear one face in one novel, a different face in the next, but which always points to the unknowable Cloud where all faces merge.

TIME AND THE TIMELESS MOMENT

In this section, the more important modes in which Time expresses itself in White's novels will be examined. At birth, the soul falls into the ocean of Time, just as it falls into that of Matter, and until its release from the body by death it must remain subject to temporal necessity. Time will first be looked at in its external manifestations, as natural time and social time. Then it will be discussed as a subjective event—psychological time—particularly in its aspect as eroder of the self. Finally, the two main ways that Time as an enemy can be overcome or redeemed will be suggested.

Natural time in White's novels operates rhythmically or in cycles. There is little sense of either evolving or degenerating natural time. The dynamic temporal theories which have proliferated since the time of Hegel, which suggest the emergence of Spirit from Matter through Time, have little relevance for White's writing. Nor, except for brief hints in *Happy Valley* and at the end of the play *Night on Bald Mountain*, do Millennial or apocalyptic theories of the end of Time figure importantly in his philosophy. The assumptions underlying natural time in his novels are closer to those of fertility myths than they are to evolutionary theories or millennial creeds. His artistic interest is in the lifetime of the individual, and within this span only the smaller movements of natural time are relevant: the alternation of day and night, the opening and closing of the seasons or the progression from childhood to old age.

Like natural time, social time is non-directional, typified by the permanence of recurrence, rather than teleology. White records the external manifestations of social change with the eye of a true novelist, but his observations are only tangentially organized around an idea of historical destination. In *The Tree of Man*, he chronicles, with great understanding and perceptiveness, the initial silence, lack of tradition and thinness of cultural texture that prevailed in Australia eighty or so years ago. Slowly he builds up the accretions of social change as the unspectacular lives of the Parkers and their neighbours grow and intertwine. But though the silence is filled, there is no necessary sense of direction. It is true that there are certain aspects of the march of material ugliness from which White recoils, in particular the slow sprawl of Sydney suburbia. The pastoral mode of *The Tree of Man* is slowly eroded by the red brick houses, just as Xanadu in *Riders in the Chariot* is destroyed and replaced by a housing estate. His depiction of this is more an expression of temperamental aversion than a theory of historical decline. He is interested principally in contrasting two ethics, and the polarity exists even in those works where the emphasis is not on change. In *The Living and the Dead* there is no less sense of the spiritual malaise of the red brick life, but no suggestion that this is physically on the increase. The sprawl appears as a matter for concern only in *The Tree of Man* and *Riders in the Chariot*. Even in these two novels the increase of suburban ugliness does not, in fact, destroy anything which has not already been renounced. Stan Parker voluntarily decides to give up most of his farm, accepting the renunciation as a spiritual necessity, while Mary Hare abandons Xanadu willingly—the bulldozers destroy only a deserted shell. Indeed, our last glimpse of Mrs Godbold is of her going up to the housing estate which has replaced Xanadu, and making friends with the denizens.

The changing forms of society are simply a setting for permanent personality types and emotional or spiritual problems. *Voss* is set almost a hundred years before the other novels but its themes are the same. The Bonners are cousins of the Armstrongs, Mrs de Courcy faces the same emptiness and practises the same antique charms as Madeleine Fisher, Laura Trevelyan is spiritually kindred to Alys Browne, Judd is another Stan Parker and Voss wrestles with the same torments as Waldo Brown. It is the permanent condition of the soul that interests White.

'"History is the reflection of spirit."' (RC p. 214) True history is not the linked chain of external events but the welling-up and overflowing of the soul. This is particularly evident in the case of war, which is an expression on the social stage of private malaise. The wars, however, play a minor part in White's thinking; his main interest is in the inner life, and the collective nightmare of war dwarfs the individual:

> 'The war years are too remote from art—from life, you might say—for any kind of artist. You have to get through them—intellectually, at least—the quickest way possible.' (Viv p. 417)

The chthonic forces that break through the surface in the general form of war are just as potent, and probably more significant, when they manifest themselves at the individual level in evil acts committed in obscure corners. This is the moral of *Riders in the Chariot*, where Himmelfarb, surviving the horrors of Nazi Germany and the extermination camp, is killed by a mob of good honest Australians. This is pointed up again in *The Solid Mandala*:

> Arthur said: 'Over in Europe they're dragging the fingernails out of all those Feinstein relatives. They're sticking whole families in ovens.'
> 'What's that to do with us? We don't put people in ovens here.'
> 'We didn't think of it,' Arthur said. (SM p. 174)

Public history is simply psychic history on a grand scale. Even in the most 'historical' of all White's novels—*Voss*—this is still true. Many of the external features of Voss's journey are based on historical fact: the incidents, landscapes, characters, even the personality of Voss himself, have much in common with the annals of the German explorer Leichhardt. It is not the external events, however, but the inner significance in which White is interested. White's true subject is not 'history' but 'legend'.

Legend is generated not by opening up new tracts of land for settlement or exploitation but by imaginative fusion of the soul of the nation with its country. This is a particularly relevant concept in a 'new' country like Australia, to whose primordial and intransigent forms the spirit of the whites has remained largely unwedded. The descent of the individual soul into the body must be paralleled by the descent of the spirit of a people into their land, experiencing completely its unknown content of beauty and terror.

Whatever human and spiritual shortcomings Voss may have, he has one quality which makes him stand out above the white huddlers on the coast. He has the vision and the courage to leave the shore and walk 'on the floor of the ocean'; he penetrates the interior as though by *droit de seigneur*. He carries the imagination of the Europeans out into the desert, and by his sufferings, his death and his merging with the animistic Dreamtime of the aboriginal inhabitants, effects a union which, without his perverse and megalomaniacal mission, could not have been achieved. His soul, in one form, stays out in the desert where he becomes a new culture hero for the blacks; in another form, through the medium of Laura Trevelyan, it returns to Sydney, to inspire those who come after.

The explorer is not alone in this creative act; with him are the artist, the saint and the martyr (whose martyrdom may be the obscure suffering of a common person that is never recorded in chronicles). The involuntary suffering of the common people and the self-sacrificing suffering of the saint both unite the soul of man with the soul of his country, letting their blood run into it in a spiritual union. The artist, on the other hand, penetrates matter with his creative intuition and, by raising it to a higher imaginative level, helps heal the breach between society and nature. This is summed up in the utterances of Laura Trevelyan:

Finally, I believe I have begun to understand this great country which we have been presumptuous enough to call *ours*, and with which I shall be content to grow since the day we buried Rose. For part of me has now gone into it. Do you know that a country does not develop through the prosperity of a few landowners and merchants, but out of the suffering of the humble? I could now lay my head on the ugliest rock in the land and feel at rest. (V p. 256)

'Oh, yes, a country with a future. But when does the future become present? This is what always puzzles me.'
'Now.'
'How—now?' asked Mr Ludlow.
'Every moment that we live and breathe, and love, and suffer, and die.'
'That reminds me, I had intended asking you about this—what shall we call him?—this familiar spirit, whose name is upon everybody's lips, the German fellow who died.'
'Voss did not die,' Miss Trevelyan replied. 'He is still there, it is said, in the country, and always will be. His legend will be written down, eventually, by those who have been troubled by it.'
'Come, come. If we are not certain of the facts, how is it possible to give the answers?'
'The air will tell us,' Miss Trevelyan said. (V pp. 477–8)

True history is not the chronicle of social change, or the recording of great public upheavals, but rather the 'legend' which is created when a people participates totally in the life of its country. For this reason, the Parkers or Arthur Brown are as significant historically as Voss. For this reason also, Patrick White's novels are themselves of profound historical importance since through the very act of writing them he has contributed to the fusion of the white mind with its land.

As well as these general and external aspects of time, White also creates a very vivid sense of inner, psychological time as it is experienced by the individual. Time future, time present and time past are living realities for the inner life. White constantly evokes, through image, suggestion and statement the presence, in an enterprise like that of Voss or in the lifetime of an individual, of the three stages of anticipation, experience and completion. We feel this strongly in *The Tree of Man*, in which the seasons, rotating from spring to winter, underpin the lives of Amy and Stan. In the first part of the book, Stan confronts an emptiness: all is latent, not yet in being. Slowly the future becomes real and Stan lives his life in the present with all its implications of love and suffering. Finally, as winter draws in, there is a mood of retrospect and nostalgia. This pattern is even more apparent in *Voss* which is constructed like a triptych around the three stages of future, present and past. In the first five chapters a sense of futurity prevails, in the face of which the present dwindles into insignificance. The central panel of the novel is dominated by the present, as expectation turns into actuality, while the closing chapters are filled with a sense of exhaustion, a sense of a cycle closed and passions spent.

White weaves these three strands of time together in the minds of his characters to create a dense and vivid sense of personal duration. Sometimes it is the present which dominates:

. . . present and future are like a dreadful music, flowing and flowing without end, and even Mrs Godbold's courage would sometimes falter as she trudged along the bank of the one turbulent river towards its junction with the second, always somewhere in the mists. (RC p. 262)

Sometimes it is the future:

But 'safe' is an optimistic word. Her hands would withdraw from the child she had put to sleep, and already the future was growing in the house, making a tangle of the present. Already she was powerless. (TM p. 114)

Sometimes it is the past:

If Amy Parker continued to sit, it was because the rose is rooted, and impervious . . . She was firmly rooted in the past, as old roses are . . . she had grown up full and milky out of the past, even her little girl must wait for roses, while nodding and stirring her mind twined again, twining through the moonlight night on which it had half-spoken, half-dreamed the rose. (TM p. 120)

Through the novels there is an immediate sense of the experience of passing time, as hope and fear, experience and memory are absorbed into the sensibility. Sometimes this is intensified to a pitch beyond psychological realism. Not only do characters expect or dread what is to come, but they also intuit or prophesy. Future traumas seem to generate waves that ripple back into the present. Anticipation turns into foresight, anxiety dreams into omens. Time appears to have a supernatural aspect that operates independently of normal laws of temporal causality. This parallels the supernatural destruction of spatial barriers that can be seen in the relationship between Voss and Laura. In *The Vivisector*, the planchette predicts the future destiny of both Hurtle and Rhoda. In *Voss*, the clasp-knife with which Voss is executed is prefigured in the butter-knife used at the Bonners' table (V p. 128) and the knife of which Turner dreams and which he later throws over the side of the *Osprey* (V p. 127, p. 132).

In *The Aunt's Story*, this intuitive awareness or foreknowledge is expressed through a technique of stylistic elision. Scenes merge into one another through images or dreams which have both a syntactical and a prophetic significance. Situations remain opaque because their emotional content is governed not by the present or the past but by an event that is is still only potential. This can be seen in the series of apparently unconnected vignettes whose unexplained emotional power is generated by the death of Theodora's father—an event that has not yet occurred (AS p. 80, pp. 87–8).

The irresistible flow of time future into time past faces all of White's characters with the problem of Time the Destroyer, eroder of happiness and negator of identity:

So she cried at times, mostly at dusk, standing at a window, when shapes have grown tender, and she herself was disintegrating, and sucked onward, the years streaming behind her like skirts in the wind, or hair. It was frightening then. Her face abandoned the mealiness of personal sorrow and became a brooding skull, or essential face. (TM pp. 254–5)

Given time, the man and woman might have healed each other. That time is not given was their one sadness. But time itself is a wound that will not heal up. (V p. 408)

The flood of time is the enemy of personal life, dragging man away from happiness and security to old age and death. Whether implicitly or explicitly, White has applied himself in all his novels to finding ways of overcoming devouring Time.

One of the classic solutions to the problem of mutability has been the belief that it can be overcome by the revitalizing power of recollection. We see the power of memory acting against the ravages of time in *Tintern Abbey, To the Lighthouse* and, of course, *A la Recherche du Temps Perdu*. It is rewarding to examine White's use of memory or recollection to see to what extent, if at all, he accepts this solution, and also to explore other dimensions of psychological time.

In *The Living and the Dead*, which is still close to the spirit of Proust, there is what might loosely be called a 'Proustian moment' towards the end, which helps Elyot through his last phase of rebirth; the smell of apples on a railway station recalls his childhood to him:

> They stood in the black smell of trains. Waiting. A basket of unnaturally complexioned apples shone near by on a stall shelf, till distance shrivelled, you smelt the atticful of summer, or under trees the grass played against the legs, the cedar pencils sharpened at eleven, spilled out into the station grime . . . Outside the sighing of an anxious piston, there was still the bay, smooth, almost circular, the glistening of red and periwinkle stones. (LD p. 332)

At the end of *The Aunt's Story*, Theodora is withering away because she has lost the vital link with her own past. Holstius comes, bringing back the memory of her father and the Man who was Given his Dinner and restores to her a lost sense of continuity:

> In the peace that Holstius spread throughout her body and the speckled shade of surrounding trees, there was no end to the lives of Theodora Goodman . . . the lives into which she had entered, making them momently dependent for love or hate, owing her this portion of their fluctuating personalities, whether George or Julia Goodman, only apparently deceased, or Huntly Clarkson, or Moraïtis, or Lou, or Zack, these were the lives of Theodora Goodman, these too. (AS pp. 299–300)

Although this is a resolution in terms of memory, it is some way from the Proustian formula. After this novel, White's approach to memory is increasingly flexible, complicated and ambivalent. In *The Tree of Man*, memory, as well as having its naturalistic function of linking man with earlier stages in his growth and giving him organic continuity, is seen both as a creative and a destructive faculty. After the war, Stan Parker is returned to his past by the simple gesture of Doll Quigley, who gives him a present of rock cakes and in doing so brings back to Stan the pristine goodness of a life he had temporarily lost (TM p. 224). But in his children we see the neurotic hell into which memory can plunge those who have severed their ties with the soil but cannot totally erase the nostalgia of the past from their minds. Sometimes memory can be repressed, as when Stan and Amy deliberately forget a moment of shared intimacy after the flood, while at other times a long forgotten trauma will assert itself, as when Stan begins to think compulsively about the old man he had seen in a tree during the same flood. There can even be a moral taint associated with the deliberate cultivation of memory, as we find it practised by Amy:

Because she was a superficial and a sensual woman, when the last confessions are made, Amy Parker was soon even thinking about that other man who had been her lover, his freckled calves, and how the suspenders had eaten in . . . How she would have liked to take other men and to have rocked with them on deep seas of passion, and to have forgotten their names, and to remember their features and their eyes, prismatically, some winter, in old age after the face had fallen back into place. (TM p. 485)

In *The Living and the Dead*, Elyot Standish was finally 'cured' by undergoing the experience of 'remembering' the entire novel, the pattern that grew out of the good moments and the bad. In *Riders in the Chariot*, Mary Hare has to undergo a more gruelling, though less systematic, ordeal by recollected trauma before she is finally allowed to sink back into the earth. Mary is an expert at repression and evasion, and must undergo trial by Mrs Jolley before she can take up her place in the Deposition. Mrs Jolley forces her to see with new eyes not only the Xanadu of the present—Mary's image of her magnificent home does not altogether coincide with the dilapidated reality—but also many forgotten incidents of her past. Many moments of paternal brutality, maternal betrayal and invidious comparison with long-legged beauties such as Helen Anthill must be re-lived. And Mary must also face, if not resolve, the problem of evil and of her own complicity in it. Mrs Jolley triggers off buried traumas, with their moral implications, even by doing something as 'innocent' as writing 'For a Bad Girl' on a cake:

'What a beautiful cake!' Miss Hare had exclaimed, with something like horror.

. . . she did sense some danger to the incorporeal, the more significant part of her . . . Except for her relationship with her father, the brief unpleasantness with William Hadkin, and the death of her poor goat, she had had little experience of evil.

Days after the lettering had been consumed, Miss Hare was haunted by the
pink cake. She must, she *would* understand it, though there were pockets of
thought which her mind refused to enter, like those evil thickets in which
might be found little agonizing tufts of fur, broken swallows' eggs or a goat's
rational skull. (RC pp. 66–7)

Many of her early experiences are dark and ambiguous; it is not essential that the moral enigmas should be resolved, only that they
should finally be brought into the light of day. This process reaches a
climax with the ritual re-enactment of the fatal ball for Cousin
Eustace, which may have marked the moment of severance between
Mary and the rest of humanity. As she participates obsessively in the
'game' that Mrs Jolley has begun, Mary allows herself to experience
totally, as she had not at the time, the difference between herself and
the conventional beauties with whom she had been compared and
found wanting. In the conversation that follows the 'dance', she is
forced by Mrs Jolley to become aware of her murderous fits which are
often associated with the appearances of the Chariot:

... but I hardly like to offer criticism, not in my position, and because we
know there are times when you are not in full possession of yourself. Even so.'
   'Full possession?' asked Miss Hare.
   So softly.
   'You will not remember an evening on the terrace,' Mrs Jolley was in a
hurry, 'Or what you said, or what you did, or how you passed out cold.'

   'I *hurt* you?'
   'I'll say. And might have done real damage if you hadn't passed right out.'
   'And I can remember *nothing*.'
   'It was a kind of fit.'
   An undulating dread threatened to drown Miss Hare.
   'I told you nothing?' . . .

   'It was about the Chariot.'

   'I will not be told lies!' Miss Hare shouted.

   'You are a wicked evil woman!' Miss Hare accused . . .

   Mrs Jolley had some difficulty in releasing the handfuls of her apron.
   'If we are two of a kind,' she mumbled.
   Miss Hare could not accept the possibility of that, and was rootling in
remote recesses for some evidence of her own election. (RC pp. 96–7)

Mary is led through labyrinths of evil memory, encountering acts
of murder that she herself may have committed, and meeting the
ghost of Helen Anthill, the mirrors of whose dress reflect only too

clearly Mary's deformity. Only after this exorcizing journey of rediscovery is she in a position to benefit from her meeting with Himmelfarb and the redemptive power of living-kindness that he generates. Her love and concern for Himmelfarb, that impels her to enter his blazing house at the risk of her own life, restores to her that necessary link with humanity that she had lost for so long. As she lies at his feet her traumas or daemons are driven out and she can finally accept the mystery of man in Christ and Christ in man:

... she wrapped and cherished the heavenly spirit which had entered her. Quite simply and painlessly, as Peg had suggested that it might. And all the dancing demons fled out, in peacock feathers, with a tinkling of the fitful little mirrors set in the stuff of their cunning thighs. And the stones of Xanadu could crumble, and she would touch its kinder dust. (RC p. 492)

In Mary's case, the encounter with traumatic or daemonic memory is not a solution to the problem of time, but only a necessary cleansing process before she can be raised up by experience of the opposite principle. Whatever the healing powers of emotions recollected in tranquillity, White is here exploring darker, more chthonic areas of the mind. In *The Solid Mandala*, he probes even deeper into this aspect of memory, showing it as persecutor, destructive as time itself. Like Mary, Waldo Brown is the victim of obsessive or daemonic memory; he does not 'remember'—he is haunted by the past. Many events in his life have been suppressed, but during his long walk with Arthur all the significant events of his past return to him, triggered off by chance images, remarks or incidents in the present. The process begins as the two old men walk out of their front gate:

'This gate, Waldo,' Arthur was saying gently, 'will fall to bits any day now.' Sighing.
He was right. Waldo dreaded it. Averted his mind from any signs of rusty iron, or rotted timber. Unsuccessfully, however. His life was mapped in green mould; the most deeply personal details were the most corroded.

Suddenly the smell of rotting wood, of cold fungus, shot up through Waldo's nose. He could hardly bear, while exquisitely needing, the rusty creaking of his memory. (SM p. 26, p. 27)

The form of Part Two is, in fact, mimetic, imitating in its fragmented and obsessive assertion of incidents from the past the disintegrated condition of Waldo's mind. Arthur's section, by contrast, develops smoothly from childhood to old age, as coherent and as unified as his personality. Throughout Waldo's section, vignettes from

his personal biography rise up to haunt him, an experience which, in
the manner of the neurotic, he finds both necessary and loathsome.
We find this same kind of autonomous assertion operating at a deeper
level than that of purely personal memory. Waldo, for much of his
life, lives in a compensatory world of fantasy, which may be linked
with a deeper, ancestral memory or collective unconscious. He lives
in two ages and occupies two roles simultaneously. On the one hand
he is in the Australian present, a neurotic and insignificant librarian,
living in a wooden shack down Terminus Road. On the other hand
there is Tallboys and the Quantrell heritage, where he lives either as
the enigmatic 'other Waldo' or as an aristocratic *grande dame*,
triumphant and disdainful.

Waldo builds up his picture of Tallboys from his mother's sherry-
soaked reminiscences, but in doing so he seems to be clothing or
exploring something that already exists in his unconscious. He seems
not so much to be learning something new as to be correcting and
confirming the details of some ancestral component (SM pp. 164–5).
His obsession with the frigid and ruthless Quantrells links him with
an evil current in human nature that bursts out in the wars, with
whose guilt Waldo feels intimately associated.

The autonomous power of this building in the mind and its phan-
tom inhabitants grows as Waldo's status in the external world
dwindles. The obsessive nature of memory reveals itself most completely when Waldo's discovery of an old dress of his mother's sparks
off an orgy of schizoid compensation at the height of which the 'external' Waldo is totally possessed by the female personification of his
personal and his collective unconscious, standing on the stairs of
Tallboys:

He need not mention names, but he could see her two selves gathered on
the half-landing at the elbow in the great staircase, designed by special cunning to withstand the stress of masonry and nerves. Standing as she had never
stood in fact, because, although memory is the glacier in which the past is
preserved, memory is also licensed to improve on life . . . There were those
who considered the eyes too pale, too cold, without realizing that to pick too
deeply in the ice of memory is to blench.

. . . His heart groaned, but settled back as soon as he began to wrench off his
things, compelled. You could only call them things, the disguise he had
chosen to hide the brilliant truth . . .

When he was finally and fully arranged, bony, palpitating, plucked, it was
no longer Waldo Brown, in spite of the birthmark above his left collarbone.
Slowly the salt-cellars filled with icy sweat, his ribs shivery as satin, a tinkle of
glass beads shattered the silence. Then Memory herself seated herself in her

chair . . . in front of the glass. Memory peered through the slats of the squint-eyed fan, between the nacreous refractions. If she herself was momentarily eclipsed, you expected to sacrifice something for such a remarkable increase in vision. In radiance, and splendour. All great occasions streamed up the gothick stair to kiss the Rings of Memory, which she held out stiff, and watched the sycophantic lips cut open, teeth knocking, on cabuchons and carved ice. (SM pp. 192–3)

This is not, of course, a triumph of memory but rather a symptom of a diseased mind, crumbling under the assaults of the unconscious. It is a far cry from the solutions of Wordsworth, Woolf and Proust. It appears from this example and the others discussed above that although White is deeply interested in the psychological and spiritual activities of memory, he does not see them as bulwarks against the erosions of time. They are a part of time, working with it to regenerate or destroy. To solve the problem of time, it is clear that we must look elsewhere than memory which is only a limited aspect of the same problem.

In the rest of this section two ways in which time is overcome through time will be suggested, the first of which is analogous to music, the second to painting.

From both Platonic and Hebraic sources the idea that time is a moving image of eternity, or that human destiny is governed by the decrees of God, has flowed into Christianity. In all of White's novels there is a strong sense of a scheme, pattern or directing Providence which all local events, either good or evil, subserve. In his earlier novels this seems closer to philosophy than to religion. The ethos of *The Tree of Man* reminds one a little of the philosophy of Spinoza, with its emphasis on the necessity of total acceptance of the cosmos, total harmonization of the individual will with the will of the universe. In the middle period, particularly in *Riders in the Chariot*, the directing hand seems much more personal, closer to the historical Jehovah of the Jews than to a metaphysical principle. Whatever the origins or emphasis, however, the implications for the individual are the same. Everything in life, from its largest panorama to its smallest coincidence, is the will of God. Here is an abstract, only latently religious formulation of the idea from *The Living and the Dead*:

There was a purpose, caught from the music, even in the personal mistakes. He did not regret these. Lying in bed, there was perhaps even an ultimate pattern, woven partly from mistakes. (LD p. 129)

It is part of this pattern that the individual should assert his own will, believe in the uniqueness of his own destiny. The irony of Voss's situation is that his very perversity, his independence of the will of God, is a manifestation of that will. Assertion of personal destiny ultimately will merge into the larger pattern. White's interest in the intimate connection between the individual and Providence is hinted at in the opening pages of *The Tree of Man*:

How much of will, how much of fate, entered into this it was difficult to say. Or perhaps fate is will. Anyway, Stan Parker was pretty stubborn. (TM p. 7)

The organic relationship between fate and will is summed up in a brief but evocative image towards the end of the novel:

... the wife of the dead man ... had brought a packet of cigarettes, and had shoved one into her mouth as if it had been food, and had blown smoke from her nose in a long trumpet.
'Did *you* ever know,' she asked, 'what you was going to do?'
'Yes,' he said with an assumed certainty.
He felt, in fact, that his own intentions had always developed like smoke. They were carried. (TM p. 456)

Although the individual will is important to the divine will, turning it from essence into existence, making it visible, as smoke makes the movements of air visible, the individual is essentially carried by something dynamic moving through him.

Time shapes itself into a pattern, as does music, according to the will of a higher creative principle. As with music, the full pattern can only be understood at the end of a lifetime—the completion of the work—when the last notes are dying away. Even the bad moments are essential. It is necessary that the initial bland tonality should be departed from. The more extreme the modulations from the tonic, the more perturbing the discords of the intermediate stage of the work, the richer and profounder will the original key be when it returns in triumph in the closing chords.

White's firm architectonic control is not simply a matter of literary form. In every novel, it can be seen as mimetic, imitating the music of time, unfolding in a pattern through which Providence is revealed. This pattern moves along through a series of good or bad moments, the episodes which make up the novels. The bad moments are traumas, contact with the principles of suffering and evil which are painful but as paradoxically necessary as the Fall. The remainder of this section will be devoted to a brief discussion of the good moments or 'epiphanies' in which the character has a fleeting experience of the Hidden God.

The concept of the 'timeless moment' has many literary ancestors, such as Wordsworth, Pater, Joyce, Proust, Woolf and Eliot. There is not room here to investigate the particular influences of White's literary forbears, though one can say that he appears closest in spirit to the T. S. Eliot of *The Four Quartets*. The discussion here will be limited to the component elements of the 'White epiphany' and their significance within the novels.

Although the timeless moments in White take different forms, they have the same rhythm and the same features. They tend to be organized around the movement of the three stages outlined in Chapter One, in which arrogance or a sense of pseudo-divinity gives way to humility or even despair, which is, in turn, replaced by a moment of Grace. Within this rhythm there are six distinguishable elements which cluster around the central event.

Firstly, these moments begin with some kind of transition in which the character moves out of his mundane setting into a condition of expectancy:

> But suddenly they had climbed out, panting and dazzled.
> 'Oh, look!' she called, pointing.
> 'That's a wheel-tree,' said Arthur.
> He could tell because Mrs Musto had shown him one. Still panting, he stood smiling, proud of the treeful of fiery wheels.
> And under the tree was standing the Chinese woman, whom he often remembered afterwards. They stood looking at one another. Then the Chinese woman, so little connected with them, or their other surroundings, turned, it seemed resentfully, and went behind some poultry sheds. There was no great reason why he should remember her, except as part of the dazzle of the afternoon. For that reason he did. (SM p. 263)

Secondly, the world of sense impressions is heightened to an almost hallucinatory pitch, although never completely obliterated:

> . . . the two people ignored each other for a moment, staring back at the material world . . . which further experience might soon remove from their lives.

> . . . a bird cupped in the grey goblet of her nest, a litter of young rabbits moving by clockwork into grass, the eyelids of a lizard denying petrification by the sun. It was perfectly still, except that the branches of the plum tree hummed with life, increasing, and increasing, deafening, swallowing them up. (RC p. 101)

Thirdly, strange emotions of love, tranquillity and fulfilment spread around the character:

Resistance had gone out of her as she lay, her head against the knees of Holstius, receiving peace, whether it was from his words, and she was not altogether sure that he spoke, or from his hands. His hands touched the bones of her head under the damp hair. They soothed the wounds. (AS p. 293)

Holstius laid his hands on, and she was a world of love and compassion that she had only vaguely apprehended. Leaves glistened down to the least important vein. (AS p. 299)

Fourthly, there is often a profound sense of communion with another or with nature:

... there will be moments of passing affection, through which the opaque world will become transparent, and of such a moment you will be able to say—my dear child. (AS p. 64)

Fifthly, mythical or archetypal resonances grow out of the particular images of the world of here and now which momentarily lift the plane of the action from the temporal to the eternal:

So, in his mind, he loaded with panegyric blue the tree from which the women, and the young man His disciple, were lowering their Lord . . . As they lowered their Lord with that almost breathless love, the first Mary received him with her whitest linen, and the second Mary, who had appointed herself the guardian of his feet, kissed the bones which were showing through the cold, yellow skin. (RC p. 490)

Finally, light—whose source is only apparently natural—suffuses the scene, and hints that this is, indeed, a moment of illumination:

Events of great importance would take place if only the moment of lightning could occur. But it did not yet seem that the little soft flashes playing about the mountaintops would gather themselves together to achieve supreme power . . . He flickered like the little bursts of lightning on the mountaintops . . .

A great fork of blue lightning gashed the flat sky . . .

Soon the land was shining whenever lightning opened its darkness. That torment of darkness, of lashing, twisted trees became rather, an ecstasy of fulfilment.

The lightning, which could have struck open basalt, had, it seemed, the power to open souls. It was obvious in the yellow flash that something like this had happened, the flesh had slipped from his bones, and a light was shining in his cavernous skull. (TM pp. 150–2)

All these elements are fused together and given their most beautiful expression in *The Eye of the Storm*, during Elizabeth Hunter's experience on Brumby Island. This, as was remarked in Chapter One, is organized around the three stages, of which the middle phase is a black night of helplessness and guilt. It is introduced by a strange interlude during which Elizabeth finds herself deserted as the storm approaches. In the following passage the importance of light, heightened sensuous perception and emotions of tranquillity and love are evident, as are the archetypal resonances of the seven black swans and, of course, the Eye itself, which recalls the Eye-Gods of mythology. What is less evident is that the swans have been connected, elsewhere in the novel, with Mrs Hunter's children, and that in the act of feeding them she is symbolically giving of herself to her children as she had never been able to in real life. It is truly a moment of communion:

... she was no longer a body, least of all a woman: the myth of her womanhood had been exploded by the storm. She was instead a being, or more likely a flaw at the centre of this jewel of light: the jewel itself, blinding and tremulous at the same time, existed, flaw and all, only by grace; for the storm was still visibly spinning and boiling at a distance, in columns of cloud, its walls hung with vaporous balconies, continually shifted and distorted.

But she could not contemplate the storm for this dream of glistening peace through which she was moved. Interspersed between the marble pyramids of waves, thousands of seabirds were at rest . . . and closer to shore there were the black swans—four, five, seven of them.

She was on her knees in the shallows offering handfuls of the sodden loaf the sea had left for her. When they had floated within reach, the wild swans outstretched their necks. Expressing neither contempt nor fear, they snapped up the bread from her hands, recognizing her perhaps by what remained of her physical self, in particular the glazed stare, the salt-stiffened nostrils, or by the striving of a lean and tempered spirit to answer the explosions of stiff silk with which their wings were acknowledging an equal.

All else was dissolved by this lustrous moment made visible in the eye of the storm . . . (ES p. 424–5)

These intense moments are to painting what the pattern of the novels is to music. The many paintings which appear in White's novels express the possible moment of epiphany in which a character is lifted out of his temporal setting and placed among the icons of eternity. Such fleeting moments occur to characters throughout their lives, as can be seen by Elyot Standish's experience at Ard's Bay or Arthur Brown's moments of dialogue with Dulcie Feinstein, but they tend to centre around two key encounters with the heart of the mystery. The first of these occurs during the height of maturity and is both a casting down and a lifting up. It humbles the individual who may have become over-confident of his self-sufficiency, but at the same time it is a foretaste, a promise and a pledge. It rewards him for his perseverance up to this point, lifts him for a moment onto a higher plane where he glimpses the numinous world behind the forms of nature, and then drops him back into the stream of becoming. Such a pledge is given to Stan Parker during the second storm quoted above, to Himmelfarb and Mary Hare in their glimpses of the Chariot, to Arthur Brown during his mandala dance and, of course, to Elizabeth Hunter on Brumby Island. It is also found in *The Vivisector*, where Hurtle has his first glimpse of the Indigod as he lies on the pavement after his first stroke. The perversity of the love of this Moment God is shown in the fact that the road to be followed after this first encounter is often more difficult than that which led up to it. If the road is followed, however, and the quester sincerely tries to live out the implications of the mystery that has been revealed, then his lifetime will be crowned by the second appearance of Grace.

The second encounter with eternity is a fulfilment of the promise, the redemption of the pledge. The Eye is once more focused on the individual, but it is now not a momentary hint but a permanent state of Being. The manner of infolding is expressed differently in the different novels, but its import is always the same. Having unfolded from its source in the Hidden God and passed through the vicissitudes of the fallen world and the rigours of temporal necessity, the soul shakes off the clay of its incarnate form and returns to its timeless source.

PART TWO

THE HUMAN WORLD

5
The Psychic Mandala

THE SOUL AND THE SELF

In this Part we turn from the principles that run through the groundswell of Being to the human personality through which these principles express themselves. This Part is organized like a mandala of which the core is the soul and the outer circumference is society. In the discussion, certain concepts will be employed to indicate different zones of the temperament. These concepts are all components of that one mysterious entity 'I'. At certain points they merge into one another in such a way that it is not always easy or even desirable to make rigid distinctions between them. But if we are to grasp the metaphysical basis of White's characterization, it is a necessary preliminary to disentangle and express as clearly and simply as possible the different meanings that the word 'I' may contain. Three basic distinctions will be made, of which each but the first is capable of further subdivision.

The ineffable core of the mandala-personal is the spark of divinity that is planted as potential in everyone at birth. This will be referred to as 'the higher soul', 'the hidden soul' or simply 'the soul'. This is the indwelling Christ of Christian mysticism or the *shecchinah* of Jewish mysticism. Surrounding this like a womb or alchemist's retort is a lower, or working soul. This will be called 'the self' or 'the core of being' and is similar to the Jungian Self that is the end-product of the individuation process. The division or rupture that occurs in this core of being is between the principles of Nous and Physis. Finally, there is the existential or phenomenological self—the subject of orthodox psychiatry and psychology—of which the potential divisions are manifold. The 'I' can be experienced as identical with any one of these three selves or with any subdivision within them. I can identify with my having self, my erotic self, my cogitating self, my social self, my core of being or with the soul. A quotation from Gabriel Marcel may

81

help pinpoint the area of religious philosophy in which Patrick White is working:

We can find no salvation for mind or soul unless we see the difference between our being and our life. The distinction may be in some ways a mysterious one, but the mystery itself is a source of light. To say 'my being is not identical with my life' is to say two different things. First, that since *I am* not my life, my life must have been given to me; in a sense unfathomable to man, I am previous to it; *I am* comes before *I live*. Second, my being is something which is in jeopardy from the moment my life begins, and must be saved; my being is at stake, and therein perhaps lies the whole meaning of life. And from this second point of view, I am not *before* but *beyond* my life. This is the only possible way to explain the ordeal of human life (and if it is not an ordeal, I do not see what else it can be). And here again, I hope very much that these words will not stir up in our minds memories of stereotyped phrases drowsily heard in the torpor too often induced by a Sunday sermon. When Keats—certainly not a Christian in the strict meaning of the word—spoke of the world as a 'vale of soul-making', and declared in the same letter of April 28th, 1819, that 'as various as the Lives of men are—so various become their souls, and thus does God make individual beings, Souls, Identical Souls, of the sparks of his own essence', he had the same idea as mine, . . .[10]

The relationships between the hidden soul, the self and the temperament are analogous to the relationships between the Hidden God, the paired principles and the phenomenal world. The soul emanates outwards through, and in turn is nourished by, the external aspects of personality. Like the Hidden God, it must express or even find itself through cleavage and pain, but although psychological and physical existence—the vehicles of the divided soul—are 'real' they exist on a lower ontological plane than the soul, and their dissolution is not necessarily the dissolution of spirit. The hidden soul is faceless, nameless and unknowable. Like the Hidden God its presence can only be surmised, but without this supposition no other psychic event in Patrick White's novels is fully explicable. There are enough hints in White's writing to make this act of faith justifiable:

. . . this ruin of an over-indulged and beautiful youth, . . . was also a soul about to leave the body it had worn, and already able to emancipate itself so completely from human emotions, it became at times as redemptive as water, as clear as morning light. (ES p. 12)

All of which has only indirect bearing on your significant life, revealed nightly in the presence of this precious wafer of flesh from which earthly beauty has withdrawn, but whose spirit will rise from the bed and stand at the open window, rustling with the light of its own reflections, till finally disintegrating into the white strands strung between the araucarias and oaks of the emergent park, yourself kneeling in spirit to kiss the pearl-embroidered hem, its cold weave the heavier for dew or tears. (ES p. 335)

The most numerous references to the soul are found in *Voss*. As the explorers move into the desert, some of them develop hallucinated or visionary awareness of the animistic desert religion of the aborigines. The soul, as it is encountered in the interior, is an almost corporeal entity—a bird, a spirit or a ghost, rather than the incorporeal, almost abstract soul of Christian theology. The visions or dreams of spirits point towards the existence of the higher soul, but their very concreteness hides as much as it reveals of its true nature:

'These dead men' the native boy explained, and it was gathered that his people lay their dead upon such platforms, and would leave them there for the spirits to depart.
'All go,' said the blackfellow, 'All.'
As he placed his hands together, in the shape of a pointed seed, against his own breast, and opened them skyward with a great whooshing of explanation, so that the silky, white soul did actually escape, and lose itself in the whirling circles of the blue sky, his smile was radiant. (V p. 260)

'The shape of a pointed seed', or of the almond, appears frequently in *Voss*, suggesting the almost biological link between generation and regeneration of the soul.

In the bird and ghost souls of *Voss*, we have already moved away from the hidden soul towards spiritism. At a slightly lower level again, there are various forms of uncanny psychic occurrences in the novels, which are, strictly speaking, parapsychological rather than religious. In *The Aunt's Story*, Theodora has the prophetic dream mentioned in the last chapter. In *The Tree of Man*, Thelma Forsdyke becomes aware through some extra-sensory intuition that her father has died. In *Riders in the Chariot*, Reha appears in dreams and visions to direct her husband. Above all, there is the strange link between Voss and Laura, which may, for much of the novel, be explained naturalistically, but, at least in the climactic chapter, must be accepted at its face value as a 'real' abnormal psychic event. Like so much else in the book, this telepathic relationship shows the blend of European and aboriginal beliefs that White creates. The German romantics, whose influences can be felt strongly in *Voss*, were fascinated by such parapsychological occurrences, while anthropologists have observed telepathic powers among the inhabitants of the Australian interior:

The Aborigine has, in fact, developed the art of contemplation to a much greater degree than most of us. He may be taking part in general conversation

... when ... he drops into a state of recollection and receptivity, lasting minutes, until he has realized who will be 'coming along' in the near future ...

Many white folk who have known their native employees well, give remarkable examples of the Aborigine's power for knowing what is happening at a distance, even hundreds of miles away ... how he could have known, they do not understand, for there was no means of communication whatever and he had been away from his own people for weeks and even months ... In any case, granted their animistic and 'dreaming' philosophy, they are quite logical, and what is more, they act on their logic and apparently seldom find it wanting.[11]

Although the relationship between Voss and Laura serves a religious end, it is in itself not religious—it demonstrates the power of the mind to transcend normally accepted physical limitations, but it does not really illuminate the nature of the soul. ESP has the same tangential connection with the hidden soul as miracles have with the Hidden God.

For a novelist, there is a more important aspect of the soul than its hidden, theological nature, ghost appearances or psychic occurrences. For existential purposes, for the business of living in the flesh and in the world, these are crucial but latent concerns. The centre of the psychic mandala as it is actually experienced in life is a core of being which has a more personal and fleshly reality than its ghostly twin. This core of being is the centre of the temperament, and is fed by the total personality, including sense impressions, fears, instincts, dreams, conscious thought and memory. It has the capacity to blaze up in response to the poetry of life, or to undergo the torments of personal suffering. It relates outwardly to the entire temperament and inwardly to the higher soul. The latter, whose mission it is to achieve unity with the Hidden God, can only fulfil its destiny by living out the implications of existence. It must emanate through the phenomenological self and enter into dialogue with the external world in both its social and its natural aspects. The core of being is the first stage in this emanation. Whereas the higher soul is faceless and, in a sense, anonymous, the working soul is tied more closely to the individuality of its possessor. It does not have a single essence but expresses itself in various vocations. Its vocation may be love of nature or love of humanity, an obsession with exploration or a gift for painting. It can inform the life of a *zaddik* or a handmaid, a simpleton or a genius. It seeks to express itself in action, but it can exist (as with Rhoda Courtney or Theodora Goodman) even when its only vocation is to be itself. What is essential is that this centre should be open, accepting completely the conditions of existence; if it is closed, as it

seems to be in most people, it will fail in its first function, which is to
nourish the higher soul within.

Those who possess this core, genius or daemon are marked off by
the intensity and genuineness of their responses to joy and to
suffering. Its existence is hinted at in *The Aunt's Story* by the image of
the Indian filigree ball:

> So they took the filigree ball and rolled it over the carpet . . . And although
> its hollow sphere was now distorted and its metal green, when rolled across the
> drawing-room carpet the filigree ball still filled with a subtle fire.
>
> 'It's silly,' said George.
> Suddenly he wanted to kick it.
> 'It's not,' said Lou.
> Her hands protected not only the Indian ball, but many secret moments of
> reflected fire. (AS pp. 14–15)

> There were the people as empty as a filigree ball, though even these would
> fill at times with a fire. (AS p. 136)

In *The Tree of Man*, Stan Parker experiences his true self as a powerful but inexpressible surge of inner poetry:

> 'The Gold Coast, eh,' said the young man.
> As if the permanence of furniture was a myth. As if other glittering images
> that he had sensed inside him without yet discovering, stirred, heaved, almost
> to the surface . . .
>
> It was as if the beauty of the world had risen in a sleep, in the crowded wooden
> room, and he could almost take it in his hands. All words that he had never
> expressed might suddenly be spoken. He had in him great words of love and
> beauty, below the surface, if they could be found. (TM pp. 34–5)

Intuitive knowledge of the existence of the core of being may lead
White's characters into wrong paths. One such false belief is that the
true self can be totally identified with the gift, vocation, genius or
daemon through which it expresses itself. The 'gift' or obsession can
take a character a long way in his discovery of the self, but it cannot
take him all the way and if it is allowed to flourish unchecked and un-
tempered by spiritual wisdom it may pervert the soul's destiny. This
can be dramatically highlighted by contrasting the two following
quotations from *The Eye of the Storm*: '. . . my gift, which is myself . . .'
(ES p. 241); '. . . myself is this endlessness.' (ES p. 551).

Another misconception is that the true self can be reached by subtraction. Several of White's characters attempt to realize themselves by amputation, trying to slice away the external, existential aspects of their lives, in order to release the core of reality. As was pointed out in Part One, this effort is self-defeating—the centre of the mandala is finally released only by first embracing existence. In *The Aunt's Story*, Theodora commits several acts of symbolic suicide in an attempt to reach a state of pure being. Holstius saves her by pointing out that reality lies not in subtraction but in the organic processes of multiplication and division. Voss, too, attempts to find himself by self-destruction. He mistakenly identifies the self with the Nous principle in his nature and is only saved when, with the assistance of Laura, Nous is married to Physis to make him a whole man. Mary Hare also toys with this heresy of reduction: 'Eventually I shall discover what is at the centre, if enough of me is peeled away.' (RC p. 57)

The production of the self, which Jung sees as analogous to the philosopher's stone, can only be achieved if the raw material of life is fed into it. The elixir can only be created if the womb of the self is fertilized, the furnace fed; there must be complete openness to the outside world. In *The Solid Mandala*, Waldo Brown—in spite of his obsession with his 'crystal core'—is a false alchemist who lets the stone slip through his fingers by keeping the core of being shut off from life. Like Voss, Waldo makes the mistake of confusing a limited aspect of the self—the Nous aspect—with the whole self. The more he nurtures his fantasy of genius, the less capable he is of realizing it:

To submit himself to the ephemeral, the superficial relationships might damage the crystal core holding itself in reserve for some imminent moment of higher idealism. Just as he had avoided fleshly love—while understanding its algebra, of course—the better to convey eventually its essence. (SM p. 183)

More than anything else these dubious overtures, such an assault on his privacy, made Waldo realize the need to protect that part of him where nobody had ever been, the most secret, virgin heart of all the labyrinth. (SM p. 191)

The self can be either developed or destroyed according to the temperament and life style of the individual. The spirals of degeneration and regeneration mentioned in Part One relate directly to the core of being. The misuse of a lifetime will corrupt and destroy it by an almost organic process, and this corruption will, in turn, destroy the potential higher soul. On the other hand, if the separate elements of the personality can be wedded one with another within the core of being, so that the word 'I' is spoken from the centre of the mandala, then this personal 'I' will itself dissolve and be transcended as the hidden soul returns to the Hidden God.

Chance has endowed the English language with the possibility of symbolizing the 'I' by the 'eye'. Most clear-sighted, reasonable people, who believe that if I think therefore I am, see only as through a glass darkly. The blind eyes of Elizabeth Hunter, through which a mineral blue will flash from time to time, are the most fitting emblem for the condition of the soul impeded in its attempts to see clearly. Its sight is obscured by a film of matter, just as the Eye is obscured by the Storm. Only when the Eye is focused on her for the last time is it implied that the scales will fall, and she will see face-to-face on a level where blindness and illumination are one.

We have now established the heart of the psychic mandala. From this point, the discussion will flow out through more external aspects of the temperament and beyond this to the relations between the individual and the external world. It will emphasize the divisions and obstacles that the soul encounters as it pulses outwards, and the nourishment it acquires as it flows back to the central organ.

THE TRAGIC CLOWN

Fundamental to White's characterization is a sense of discrepancy between the core of being and the temperament through which it must express itself. The goblet is seldom adequate for the elixir that it contains. As the soul moves out from the centre it is impeded and distorted by limitations and imperfections of mind, emotion or body. Existence is never adequate to express the pure poetry of essence.

Unlike the Greek sculptors, who attempted to create a perfect harmoney of idea and form, White emphasizes the pathetic incongruity of inner and outer. This accounts for the constant sense of the ludicrous, the ironic and the grotesque which surrounds his characters even when they are at an extreme point of suffering or ecstasy. In pure tragedy, as with Sophocles, and pure comedy, as in Dante's *Paradiso*, irony is discarded to be replaced by complete congruity of spirit, emotion and style. There is no such unmediated flow in White. His style is at its most wry and bathetic as the zenith or nadir is reached. It is important to realize that this irony is not directed at the spirit, nor is it intended to undercut or pervert the meaning and importance of the events. It is a reflection of his constant and inescapable sense of the imperfection and limitation of the human vessel, the inherent inadequacy of form to convey the full implications of idea.

The impediments that the temperament opposes to the core can be

seen in the case of Theodora Goodman, incapable of expressing the
'flaming moments', and in Stan Parker who never succeeds in writing
down the poetry that swells inside him. In *Voss*, the Faustian or
Luciferian resonances of the German are undercut by an essentially
limited and nasty temperament; Voss is ludicrous rather than terri-
ble. Mary Hare has visions of God, but her frame is so frail that, like
some little wood sprite driven mad by the presence of Pan, she is
bludgeoned and terrified, rather than uplifted, by her experience.
Arthur Brown's mission of responsibility and love is turned aside and
frustrated by the lumbering mind and clumsy frame which have been
tied to his dedicated soul.

This aspect of characterization is expressed through images of
clowns, harlequins, dolls and pierrots. It lies behind the references to
circuses, vaudeville, pantomime and farce. These sum up the sense
that man, in his highest aspirations to love or lowest depths of
suffering, is still inescapably encumbered by the inadequacy of personality. This image pattern is found in its relation to love in *The Solid
Mandala*:

The *pierrot d'amour* on the cover certainly conveyed less expectancy, less of
the slightly scented breathlessness of the afternoon when Dulcie had explained
about the *pierrot* on Mrs Musto's bottle.
So Arthur sat, and as the clanking tram flung the passengers together, composed his own version of a song. (SM p. 248)

'Who am Ieeehhh?
Guess! Guess! *Guesss!*'

'*Peerrot d'amor*
At half-past four,
That's what I am!
How the leaves twitter—
And titter!
No one is all that dry,
But Ieeehhh!' (SM p. 134)

In its relationship to suffering, the clown image appears in *Riders in
the Chariot*, in a vignette that pointedly precedes the crucifixion of
Himmelfarb:

'Oh, I say, a circus!'

Most comical was one of the clowns who pretended to enact a public
hanging on the platform of a lorry . . .
'They will kill the silly bugger yet!' screamed one of the grannies . . .

It did seem as though the clown's act had been played out at last, for a second procession ... had united precipitately with the first ... the second procession was seen to be that of an actual funeral ...

As the clown spun at the end of his rope, and the little property coffin hesitated on the brink of the lorry ... a woman rose in the first funeral car, or stuffed herself, rather, in the window; a large, white woman—could have been the widow—pointing, as if she had recognized at last in the effigy of the clown the depth, and duration, and truth of grief ...

It had not been established whether the clown was dead, or again shamming, when the interlocked processions dragged each other round the corner and out of sight. (RC pp. 453–5)

After a brief and ribald expression of this motif in *The Vivisector*, where Hurtle Duffield paints 'The Old Fool Having Bladder Trouble', it is developed at length in *The Eye of the Storm*. The sad, masochistical little Jewess Lotte Lippmann expresses it in all its twentieth century hopelessness and desolation during her vaudeville song-and-dance routines for Mrs Hunter and also in her own pathetic life and death:

'*Wenn Mutter in die Menage ritt,*
Wie jauchzt' mein Herz auf Schritt und Tritt
Hoppla, hoppla, tripp, trapp, trapp ...'

'*Es ist'ne Welt für leere Laffen,*
Ein Zirkus mit dressierten Affen
Die Löwen und die Löwenkätzchen
Die Dame ohne Unterleib,
Die Hohe Schul' mit allen Mätzchen,
Was ist es schon? Ein Zeitvertreib!' (ES p. 444)

For Lotte there appears to be no escape from the masquerade of life. The case of Sir Basil Hunter, however, suggests that there may be a resolution to the pantomime. To himself—and often to others—Basil is not so much the Great Man as the Eternal Fool. Basil's foolishness constantly flickers around him, undercutting his pretensions: '"... I'm the one who's the fool!"' (ES p. 509); '... still the FOOL.' (ES p. 595). The identification becomes complete in the dream sequence quoted in Chapter Three and in the realization that follows the dream: 'Compose a wire, then, to the Jacka, if he could get his tongue round the significant word. (FOOL ...)' (ES p. 595). The Fool, in fact, has a crucial role to play in Basil's quest to create the unplayable Lear:

... this is why He is unplayable by actors anyway at those moments when the veins are filled with lightning the Fool flickering in counterpoint like conscience ... (ES pp. 272-3)

Lear, as well as being the most powerful figure in tragedy, is also a foolish old man, and if Basil is to achieve him it is necessary that the fool as well as the lightning should expose him for what he is. Basil's confrontation with the fool and the panto suggests that Lotte Lippmann's travesty world need not be a cul de sac. The black comedy of human folly and inadequacy can be transcended by the very act of acceptance, as long as this acceptance is coupled with a vision or dream of a possibly attainable higher peak. It is those who have never accepted the motley who are truly ludicrous.

This section has tried to bring out an area of White's artistic temperament, an area which he has in common with such twentieth century household names as Picasso, Kafka and Schönberg. It is important to stress that White's sense of the ludicrous elements in the human situation is not generated by his consciousness of the Void. It is not the meaninglessness of the universe and the futility of all human enterprise that makes man absurd. On the contrary, man's absurdity exists in the face of a fullness of Being so vast that his pretensions can only be seen as comic. The clown's mask in White does not conceal a void. It is stretched over a plenitude so rich and charged with meaning that no human face is adequate to express it.

THE GREAT SPLINTERING

Outside the core of being, the inner lives of Patrick White's characters exist in a state of considerable fragmentation and disorder. People are divided within and often against themselves, dominated by one function and repressing others. The will, the conscience, the instincts, the social facade or the unconscious assert themselves, suppressing or ignoring other faculties or entering into conflict with them. The discussion that begins in this section will continue in various forms throughout the rest of Part Two. Even so, it is impossible to explore all the complexities of White's psychology. The analysis will concentrate mainly on the area where psychology and metaphysics join hands. The emphasis will mainly be on the spiritual functions and dysfunctions of the process of psychic splintering as it is suggested by the following quotation:

Only de Santis realizes that the splinters of a mind make a whole piece. Sometimes at night your thoughts glitter; even de Santis can't see that, only yourself: not see, but know yourself to be a detail of the greater splintering. (ES p. 93)

The various components of the fragmented personality are almost always personified as some significant figure in the environment, so that personalities are intimately locked together. Characters project their inner life onto others, or have fragments of another's personality lodged in theirs. This process can take place at any level of personality, from superficial imitation of another's manners and tones of voice, to discovery of the Christ within in the form of a friend. The progressively deeper possibilities of this mode of psychic symbolism are suggested briefly in the following examples. Rhoda Courtney infuriates her brother by borrowing from time to time the inflections of their mother's voice, while Hurtle himself carries all his family in his memory, from which they rise on occasions to haunt him. Reha accompanies Mordecai Himmelfarb in dreams, while Amy Parker projects her wish-fulfilment fantasies on Madeleine. Theodora Goodman discovers many aspects of her own nature in the occupants of the Hôtel du Midi (the 'many lives of Theodora Goodman') and later projects a personification of her own *animus* onto the figment of Holstius. Doll Quigley is possessed, like an unhappy and unwilling medium, by the ghost of her brother, as is Jackie by Voss's spirit. Mrs Poulter discovers the Word in the flesh of Arthur Brown, as Mrs Godbold, Mary Hare and Alf Dubbo have Christ made real for them by their relationships with the crucified Jew.

Many of White's novels, at least at one level, can be read almost as psychic allegories. The works can be thought of as taking place within the being of macrocosmic Man—the Author Himself. The interactions of the characters can thus be seen as the interplay between the different faculties of this larger, unspoken character. In *The Ham Funeral*, the stage is set out like an exposed soul, of which the four characters are the four dominant functions; the nascent 'I' is the Young Man, who is finally born into true existential selfhood through interacting with the three other sides of himself. The action of *The Living and the Dead* all takes place within the mind of Elyot Standish, aspects of which are exposed and explored in the lives of the other characters. At the end, all these lives fold back again into the central consciousness which has finally been germinated by their fruitful conjunction. Theodora's 'I' divides into a multiple existence in Part Two of *The Aunt's Story* and through the interaction of the parts comes to a deeper understanding of the experiences of her earlier life. The four Riders in *Riders in the Chariot*, like Blake's four Zoas, may be

regarded as four aspects of one Cosmic Man—the Jewish Man Kadmon or the Christian Christ Pantocrator. Among many other things,
the twin brothers in *The Solid Mandala* represent in almost Taoist
terms the higher and lower souls of the same body, the one rising to
become a kind of god, the other sinking down into the soil:

> The body is activated by the interplay of two psychic structures: first, *hun*,
> which, because it belongs to the yang principle, I have translated as animus,
> and secondly, *p'o*, which belongs to the yin principle, and is rendered by me as
> anima. Both ideas come from observation of what takes place at death . . . The
> anima was thought of as especially linked with the bodily processes; at death it
> sinks to the earth and decays. The animus, on the other hand, is the higher
> soul; after death it rises in the air, where at first it is still active for a time and
> then evaporates in ethereal space, or flows back into the common reservoir of
> life . . . The animus is bright and active, the anima is dark and earth-bound.[12]

   Once we have pointed out this possible level of interpretation, it is
immediately necessary to qualify it. The novels are not just psy-
chomachia, with each character representing merely one aspect of the
soul. It is perhaps better to say that the characters themselves see things
in these terms, and that their perceptions, while being true up to a
point, may, in fact, falsify the full complexity of the emotional lives of
others. The characters, rather than the author, allegorize those
around them in order to give body to a portion of their own nature.
Returning to *The Living and the Dead*, for instance, the Standishes,' servant Julia Fallon plays an important symbolic role for both Eden and
Elyot, restoring them to the innocence and simplicity with which they
had lost contact. What is hidden from them, however, is the other side
of Julia's nature. They do not see the perplexity and frustration which
her very simplicity forces upon her. Elyot is cursed with literacy and
'knowingness'; Julia is trapped within the limitations that her 'admirable' illiteracy imposes on her. She experiences, and is tormented
by, the full reality of the condition which others, more sophisticated
than she, sentimentalize. By the end of the book, she is so tormented by
frustration, confusion and jealousy that she has become almost evil,
while remaining a touchstone of primitive goodness for the oblivious
Elyot.
   This point is made because some readers seem confused in the later
novels, particularly in *Voss*, about the Christian symbolism; being unable to resolve the question: 'Who is the Christ-figure?' they accuse
White himself of confusion. In fact, nobody is precisely a 'Christ-
figure', while everyone contains a little bit of the divine archetype. In
situations where a parallel is set up between the particular events of

the novel and the legend of Christ, this divine spark is stirred, brought to consciousness, and projected by the characters themselves onto those involved. This is made quite clear, for instance, in the death of Palfreyman. Palfreyman is no more (and no less) 'Christ' than anyone else in the book, but in his manner of dying he arouses the divine image that has been latent in the memories of the onlookers and makes it potent and unforgettable:

... the members of the expedition were so contorted by apprehension, longing, love or disgust, they had become human again. All remembered the face of Christ that they had seen at some point in their lives, either in churches or visions, before retreating from what they had not understood, the paradox of man in Christ, and Christ in man. (V p. 364)

In *Riders in the Chariot*, Himmelfarb becomes the chief activator of the Christ principle in those around him. Those who crucify and those who testify are projecting latent psychic content on him. It is the characters themselves who create the allegory, attempting to reject or release, to deface or beautify the most important part of their own souls. The miracle play that they enact at Easter does not violate the conventions of literary realism as all involved have been acquainted, through their culture, with the parts they are compelled to play; their self-identifications flow naturally from the nature of the event as it unfolds.

The splitting of the personality into different components, and the personification of those components, immediately suggests a certain schizoid tendency in White's writings. *The Aunt's Story* makes controlled literary use of schizophrenia in both the phantasmagoria of Part Two and the appearance of Holstius in Part Three, while the novel as a whole is an astonishingly vivid and accurate study of the schizoid disintegration that can result from ontological insecurity. In his short stories *The Burnt Ones*, White once more investigates the problem of the psychotic personality, particularly as it is generated by the relationship between a dominant mother and a recessive child. These sketches are developed into the full-length portrait of Waldo Brown. But personality splitting in White's novels is not purely or necessarily a matter of schizophrenia; it can be pathological or therapeutic according to the end it serves. The appearance of another person within may be obsessional and disruptive, as it is in the case of Jackie, but it can also be redemptive if the figure gives life to a necessary but hitherto dormant part of the psyche.

Four examples will be given of how splitting and personification can work for either redemption or damnation, two from *Riders in the Chariot* and two from *The Solid Mandala*. In the former novel, Harry Rosetree is divided against his own nature, repressing the Jewish element in his personality, which is not only his past and his race but is also the spiritual component of his own psyche. Roused at Passover by the smell of cinnamon and the presence of Himmelfarb, the ghost of his father emerges from Harry's unconscious, tormenting him by pointing out that he was the one who should have been the first to greet the Messiah. The resident father-figure in Rosetree's soul torments the conscience-stricken apostate to the point where, after a belated attempt to remedy his betrayal by giving Himmelfarb a Jewish burial, he commits suicide. Alf Dubbo, on the other hand, who is also divided against himself, manages to resolve the schism and achieve spiritual fulfilment. Alf is torn between his instinctual, chthonic nature and a higher consciousness which for much of the book remains inaccessible to him:

His mind was another matter, because even he could not calculate how it might behave, or what it might become once it was set free. In the meantime, it would keep jumping and struggling, like a fish left behind in a pool—or two fish, since the white people his guardians had dropped another in. (RC p. 393)

Although both the teachings and the temperament of Timothy Calderon and Mrs Pask are of dubious spiritual integrity, they create an awareness in Alf of the possibility of that 'ambitious abstraction'—Christ—which once acknowledged never leaves him in peace. Through his own limitations and the inadequacies of others, he cannot reconcile his instinctual nature with his 'pastor conscience', until his silent dialogues with Ruth Godbold, Mary Hare and Himmelfarb, and his participation in the Crucifixion and Deposition, allow him to realize that love and goodness can really exist in the flesh and not just in theory.

Although he still cannot act to save the Jew and has a bitter sense of betrayal that links him with Peter, he can bear witness through paint and achieve the same true self or Christhood that is granted to the other three Riders. It is significant that the 'Christ' he paints is not only Himmelfarb; it is also Alf Dubbo:

If Dubbo portrayed the Christ darker than convention would have approved, it was because he could not resist the impulse. Much was omitted, which, in its absence, conveyed. It could have been that the observer himself contributed the hieroglyphs of his own fears to the flat, almost skimped figure, with the elliptical mouth, and divided, canvas face, of the Jew-Christ. (RC p. 511)

An important aspect of personality division, that has already been touched on several times, is the split within the self of Nous and Physis. The idea of androgyny appears repeatedly in the novels. One thinks of Theodora Goodman and her many masculine attributes, of Voss and his struggle against the woman inside, of Himmelfarb who carries Reha under his left breast, of Hurtle Duffield who plays the female role in many of his sexual relationships and 'gives birth' in old age to Kathy Volkov. The concept of the hermaphroditic self receives its most complete expression in *The Solid Mandala*. In Waldo Brown, the division between the masculine and feminine is never healed; throughout his life he remains a victim of his bi-sexuality. Waldo obstinately and neurotically asserts his masculinity, despising Arthur for being a 'fat, helpless female'. His very denial of the female component in his nature, however, makes him most vulnerable to its assaults. As he grows older, denied more and denying more, he increasingly falls prey to the autonomous assertions of his own *anima*. This reaches its climax in the transvestite scene quoted in an earlier chapter. Waldo identifies himself from time to time with Tiresias, but unlike Tiresias, he never learns wisdom from his encounter with the female principle. Arthur's poem, which forces Waldo to face Physis directly, destroys him.

Arthur is also interested in Tiresias, but unlike Waldo he never experiences his hermaphroditic condition as a lethal schism. Instead, he uses it to explore the true nature of both his own self and that of other people. He is excited and fascinated whenever he comes across the phenomenon of bi-sexuality, accepts it without reservation or shame, and through this very acceptance achieves a unity of personality unknown to his schizoid twin. His interest in Tiresias begins in childhood:

Then there was that other bit, about being changed into a woman, if only for a short time. Time enough, though, to know he wasn't all that different. (SM p. 224)

The idea of the spiritual hermaphrodite is presented to him in later life when he is reading in the library:

On one occasion, in some book, he came across a message . . .
'As the shadow continually follows the body of one who walks in the sun, so our hermaphroditic Adam, though he appears in the form of a male, nevertheless always carries about with him Eve, or his wife, hidden in his body.'
He warmed to that repeatedly after he had recovered from the shock. (SM pp. 281–2)

The difference between the attitudes of Arthur and Waldo to this potentially dangerous subject is highlighted by this interchange between the brothers:

'If you want to know, I was thinking about Tiresias,' Arthur said to interest him. 'How he was changed into a woman for a short time. That sort of thing would be different, wouldn't it, from the hermaphroditic Adam who carries his wife about with him inside?'
Then Waldo took him by the wrists.
'Shut up!' he ordered. 'Do you understand? If you think thoughts like these, keep them to yourself, Arthur. I don't want to hear. Any such filth. Or madness.' (SM p. 283)

The final resolution of the problem of the spiritual hermaphrodite is suggested in this last quotation, in which male and female are united at the heart of the mandala:

... for a moment she was pretty certain she saw their two faces becoming one, at the centre of that glass eye, which Arthur sat holding in his hand. (SM p. 313)

At every level of personality we find the occurrence of splitting, in which fragments of others are embedded in the temperament, or psychic content is projected onto another. Where these different components cannot be reconciled, the personality eventually disintegrates or collapses into chaos, which may end in schizophrenia or even daemonic possession. When they can be made conscious and reconciled, however, they may finally harmonize and consolidate in the core of being, from which the higher soul will finally be born.

IDENTITY

All of White's characters, explicitly or implicitly, are groping to find some satisfactory answer to the existential or ontological question: 'Who am I?' Threatened by chaos within and without, they must find some mode of 'being there' in the world that will allow them to say with confidence 'I am I'. 'I am' is not the simple assertion it appears on the surface. It can torment a person to the point of madness, and it is amenable to a variety of false applications.

The problem of finding and maintaining a stable identity in the face of a hostile environment is at its most acute in the early works when, presumably, the theme was most personal to the young artist himself. It reaches its climax in *The Aunt's Story*—a novel that was written by an expatriate wrestling with the problem of returning for good to Australia. Although the writing of this book precedes the work of R. D. Laing by over a decade, it may be useful to begin a discussion of Theodora Goodman's predicament with two brief quotations from *The Divided Self*, since they illuminate so vividly the source of her madness:

> A man may have a sense of his presence in the world as a real, alive, whole, and in a temporal sense, a continuous person. As such, he can live out into the world and meet others: a world and others experienced as equally real, alive, whole and continuous.[13]

> The term schizoid refers to an individual the totality of whose experience is split in two main ways: in the first place, there is a rent in his relation with his world and, in the second, there is a disruption of his relation with himself. Such a person is not able to experience himself 'together with' others or 'at home in' the world, but, on the contrary, he experiences himself in despairing aloneness and isolation; moreover, he does not experience himself as a complete person but rather as 'split' in various ways, perhaps as a mind more or less tenuously linked to a body, as two or more selves, and so on.[14]

(The application of these remarks to the problems touched on in the preceding section is too evident to need further amplification. Indeed, there is no better gloss on all of White's early writings up to and including *The Ham Funeral* than *The Divided Self* and its central theory of 'ontological insecurity'.)

Theodora's sense of identity is sustained by a few brief positive moments or relationships. In Part One, we find such reality-giving moments in her early awareness of the beauty of roses, and in her relationships with Father, the Man who was Given his Dinner, Moraïtis and, above all, the 'spirit child' she bears Moraïtis—her niece Lou. Around the precarious core that these create, vast areas of personality are eroded, either by the negative attitudes of others—particularly her mother—or else by her own attempts at self-annihilation. A poignant and possibly crucial early trauma is recorded in the following quotation:

> Once there were the new dresses that were put on for Mother's sake.
> 'Oh,' she cried, 'Fanny, my roses, my roses, you are very pretty.'
> Because Fanny was as pink and white as roses in the new dress.
> 'And Theo,' she said, 'All dressed up. Well, well. But I don't think we'll let you wear yellow again, because it doesn't suit, even in a sash. It turns you sallow.' Mother said.

So that the mirrors began to throw up the sallow Theodora Goodman, which meant who was too yellow. Like her own sash. She went and stood in the mirror at the end of the passage, near the sewing room which was full of threads, and the old mirror was like a green sea in which she swam, patched and spotted with gold light. Light and the ghostly water in the old glass dissolved her bones. The big straw hat with the little yellow buds and the trailing ribbons floated. But the face was the long, thin yellow face of Theodora Goodman, who they said was sallow. She turned and destroyed the reflection, more especially the reflection of the eyes by walking away. They sank into the green water and were lost. (AS pp. 26–7)

Theodora learns that she is worthless in the eyes of 'normal', successful people, and that the few positive people in her life are also undervalued. As already hinted by the end of the above quotation, she is forced in paradoxical self-defence to commit acts of 'suicide'; negating her own existence so that it might not be hurt or destroyed from without. She begins a quest to destroy 'the monster Self'. This is seen in the following passage in which she shoots a little hawk with which she had identified, and, in doing so, wounds the vanity of Frank Parrott (who missed it) and thereby loses the small possibility she might have had of marrying him:

Now she took her gun. She took aim, and it was like aiming at her own red eye . . . And she fired. And it fell.
'There,' laughed Theodora, 'it is done.'
. . . She felt exhausted, but there was no longer any pain. She was as negative as air.

. . . I was wrong, she said, but I shall continue to destroy myself, right down to the last of my several lives. (AS pp. 73–4)

The death of Theodora's mother grants her the 'freedom' for which, during her years of spinster bondage, she had craved, but it is a strange and disembodied freedom which solves nothing. It is to Lou that Theo turns, for it is above all Lou who confers identity on her. Lou gives her a role in the external world, making her an Aunt, and also, through the similarity of their features and their mutual dissimilarity from others, ratifies her existence. The relationship with Lou, with its shared affection and physical intimacy, also allows Theodora to feel the reality and meaningfulness of her own body:

It was Lou, whose eyes could read a silence, and whose thin yellow face was sometimes quick as conscience, and as clear as mirrors. Theodora loved Lou. *My niece.* It was too intimate, physical, to express. Lou had no obvious connection either with Frank or Fanny. She was like some dark and secret place in one's own body. And quite suddenly Theodora longed for them to bring the children, but more especially Lou, when they came to town for the funeral. Since her mother's death, she could not say with conviction: I am I. But the touch of hands restores the lost identity. The children would ratify her freedom. (AS p. 11)

But the presence of death in the house frightens her niece and creates a barrier between them that cannot be passed. Theodora realizes, as Part One ends, that there is no real connection between herself and the lives of others, and her sense of total loneliness begins to blossom imperceptibly into madness:

> The child shivered for the forgotten box, which she had not seen, but knew.
> 'If I do not die,' she said.
> Theodora looked down through the distances that separate, even in love. If I could put out my hand, she said, but I cannot . . . There is no lifeline to other lives. I shall go, said Theodora, I have already gone. The simplicity of what ultimately happens hollowed her out. She was part of a surprising world in which hands, for reasons no longer obvious, had put tables and chairs. (AS p. 137)

Part Two of *The Aunt's Story* is one of the most delightful and also one of the most puzzling passages that White has written. On a common sense reading, we find Theodora arriving at a hotel in the south of France and participating in the lives of the other lodgers through a mixture of imagination, intuition, telepathy and, perhaps, a little lunacy. She has already shown her powers of empathy in Part One, when she participates in other lives, like those of the little hawk or Moraïtis, and what happens in Part Two is a simple, if startling, extension of this capacity. But there is another current of evidence in the book that suggests that the unreality of events in Part Two is not limited to Theodora's vicarious experience of the lives of others but extends to all of this section of the novel; it is possible that all the incidents, characters and even the Hôtel du Midi itself are no more than the creations of Theodora's ebullient but untrustworthy mind. This latter interpretation raises a vexing question: if the hotel and its inhabitants do not exist, then where exactly is the corporeal Theodora while they are being dreamed? The arguments for and against these two possible readings cannot be entered into here. But one can say that neither is true, neither is false, and that they are mutually incompatible. For that reason we must accept.

Theodora's experiences in the Hôtel du Midi, like those of Elyot in the deserted house in Ebury Street, are psychotherapeutic. This psychotherapy is not directional, does not reveal one psychological

truth. It is simply a vivid re-enactment of all the experiences in the
first part. During this re-enactment all the latent emotional content of
the events of her earlier life is laid bare. In Part One, she tended to
anaesthetize her full emotional responses in order to avoid suffering.
In Part Two, the vivisector is at work without the anaesthetic. We find
her, for example, re-living the loss of Frank Parrott through the
experiences of Sokolnikov, experiencing the ferocious knot of love-
hate with Lieselotte and Wetherby, or sharing the spurious delights of
having a fantasy child with Mrs Rapallo. But underlying all these
relationships there lies one nagging dread—the dread of non-
existence, of having no identity:

> She . . . took out objects of her own, to give the room her identity and justify
> her large talk of independence . . . All these acts, combined, gave to her some
> feeling of permanence . . . Lying . . . in sleeping cars . . . she had recalled the
> features of relations. These did give some indication of continuity of being.
> But even though more voluble, they were hardly more explanatory than the
> darning egg or moist sponge with which she invested each new room. . . . she
> could not escape too soon from the closed room . . . avoiding the brown door,
> of which the brass teeth bristled to consume the last shreds of personality,
> when already she was stripped enough. (AS pp. 114–15)

> I am preparing for bed, she saw. But in performing this act for the first time,
> she knew she did not really control her bones, and that the curtain of her flesh
> must blow, like walls which are no longer walls . . . her identity became uncer-
> tain. She looked with sadness at the little hitherto safe microcosm of the dar-
> ning egg . . . (AS p. 206)

The most important figure in Part Two is Katina Pavlou, as Lou
Parrott had been the most important in Part One. Katina is, in fact,
Lou's *avatar*. The events of Part Two mirror, in an amplified and distorted form, the rhythm of Part One. It begins with hope and ends
with desolation; the hope that begins it is born of the desolation that
ended Part One. Theodora's first fantasy involvement is her
experience of the moment of death in close, almost erotic intimacy
with Katina. The fear of death that had created the barrier between
Theodora and Lou now becomes the bond that unites her with
Katina. But as the section moves towards its nadir, Theodora 'loses'
Katina just as inevitably as she had lost Lou, though this time it is not
the fear of death but Katina's sexual initiation (another form of death)
that separates them. The close link between the Theodora–Lou and
the Theodora–Katina relationships is shown by the fact that it was the
following unspectacular, earth-shaking letter from Lou that began

the unrolling of events that led to Theodora's estrangement from Katina:

> . . . But I cannot see, from experience, that there is anything wrong with nuns. In fact, I love Sister Mary Perpetua. She has the loveliest, the saddest face. On my birthday she gave me a bag of aniseed balls and a little wooden cross. Sometimes in the afternoon we sit together, and watch the boats, and then I feel that I shall *never ever* have such a friendship ever again. (AS p. 228)

Lou, who confers identity, who creates that institution—an Aunt—could never, ever have another friend like Sister Mary Perpetua. It is after this blow that Theodora 'destroys' the Hôtel du Midi and begins her return journey to Australia which for her has now become Abyssinia, the land of the dead.

In Part Three, where the seeds of madness finally blossom into the full flower, Theodora realizes hopelessly that there is no place for her in her native land, or anywhere:

> Although she was insured against several acts of violence, there was ultimately no safeguard against the violence of personality. This was less controllable than fire. In the bland corn song, in the theme of days, Theodora Goodman was a discord. Those mouths which attempted her black note rejected it wryly. (AS p. 274)

Leaving her train at some anonymous spot in the USA, she once more applies herself to the destruction of the monster Self. Suicide is the last creative act of the threatened soul. She throws away her handbag, her tickets, and even adopts a false name. She is accepted by the Johnsons on her own terms, but the 'violence of personality' of even these simple, honest folk drives Theodora out to the lonely shack where she makes pathetic efforts to parody the activities of normal, sane housewives. But she is hounded from this refuge by the well-meaning Johnsons, and flees like a hunted animal down to the spring. Here, if her unconscious had allowed, she would have dissolved the last remnants of identity and sanity in the eternal water. But her unconscious does not allow. The same fantasy power that earlier had led her along the paths of madness now comes to the rescue and, at the last minute, works to cure her. Holstius, a familiar compound ghost of all the meaningful men and incidents of her early life, intervenes. First in the cabin and then in the woods, the combination of his abstract words of wisdom and his warm, physical presence restores Theodora to a continuity of being that she thought was lost for ever. He does not lead her into new realms of madness or vision, but gives her the courage to return to humanity. His appearance allows Theodora to say 'I am I' with confidence from a deeper level of personality than she had ever known. The last glimpse we have of Theodora is of her once more wearing her hat, upon which flourishes a now confident black rose—confident even of its right to doubt.

After *The Aunt's Story*, with its existential problems and its existential solution, there is a marked change in the tone of Patrick White's novels. This change may tentatively be linked with two important biographical developments. Between *The Aunt's Story* and *The Tree of Man*, White finally returned to Australia for good, and established an organic bond with his country by setting up a farm at Castle Hill ('Sarsaparilla'). Also during this period, the latent religious content of the early works came to the surface and infused into *The Tree of Man* and all succeeding novels a spiritual certainty that was lacking before. The return to Australia and the intensification of the religious factor greatly decrease the sense of existential uncertainty, and give new confidence in the strength of the core of being. The 'I' that is the subject of all the books after *The Aunt's Story* is an ontological, not a phenomenological, entity. The quest for identity is no longer the major theme of any of the novels. In spite of the flickerings, uncertainties, doubts, divisions and sufferings of the external temperament, characters like Stan Parker, Voss, Laura, Himmelfarb, Arthur, Hurtle and Elizabeth Hunter have a sense of certainty and purpose that protects them from the inroads of doubt that torment Theodora Goodman. The quest for identity remains an important preoccupation for some minor characters all of the time and for some major characters for a little of the time, but it is not the central dynamic of the writing. White always uses his profound understanding of and sympathy with identity problems to create such characters as Harry Robarts and Basil Hunter, but this awareness is now woven in as one strand of characterization among many. Even Hurtle Duffield, whose defensive cry: 'I am an artist!' sounds hollow in his own ears at those points where his deficiencies as a human being in every other way have been exposed, has a certainty about his gift and, finally, a conviction about God that renders him immune from existential assaults. Patrick White's major characters have two important experiences to live out, neither of which is, strictly speaking, a quest for identity. The first is the need to discover and to unfold their destiny as they understand it. The second, which is intimately linked with the first but not identical, is the need to achieve salvation. Thus, for example, Voss is not 'looking for himself' in the desert. He knows who he is (Gott!) and is simply confirming his destiny. His journey may provide others like Judd, Harry or

Frank with an opportunity to find themselves, but for Voss it is a voyage of ratification, not of discovery. Needless to say, his premises are faulty, but this is irrelevant to his confidence in them. The second crucial life experience for Voss—that of finding Grace—is also not the object of a quest. On the contrary, it is thrust upon his obstinate and unwilling soul by Laura. Whatever quests there are in White, the quest for identity is, for the major characters, the least relevant. Pursuit of the secular vocation and thirst for God are their main preoccupations.

The important division in the novels is between a small group of characters who have a sense of selfhood that is generated by a belief in their core of being and those who speak the 'I' from one limited aspect of their external personalities. Most of White's characters outside the inner circle tend to identify the 'I' with their thinking, their doing, or their having. They fortify themselves in the rational, social ego, and from this citadel they try to construct a sense of reality of both the nature and possibilities of the external world and the meaning and processes of their own psyches. Secular humanism, based on the Cartesian formula 'I think therefore I am', is, for White, one of Australia's worst spiritual sicknesses. The conscious, rational mind and the reality it attempts to structure and define are epiphenomena, and to identify the self with them is to ignore nine-tenths of experience. There are many portraits in White of the plight of the rationalist—whose rationalism may appear as common sense 'reasonableness' or the clever 'knowingness' of the socialite. There are the two rationalists Mr Brown and Mr Feinstein of *The Solid Mandala*, desperately trying to avert their gaze from the lethal numinous world that floats around them. There is Boo Davenport who uses her lively intellect to keep life at arm's length, and the clock-obsessed Wyburd and Alfred Hunter whose passion for chronological time suggests a spiritual incapacity to cope with more fluid forms of duration. In Judd, we find a very interesting, and also very sympathetic, picture of the limitations of the rationally defined self. Like the others, Judd is a quester, but his questing is limited by the limitations of navigational equipment. He is almost obsessed with his compasses, and when the last is broken so that distance can no longer be controlled or space charted, he turns back, leaving the three extremely unreasonable visionaries to explore areas that the intellect cannot reach. In all of the novels between *The Living and the Dead* and *The Vivisector*, White chooses characters who either cannot or will not mediate their experience through the rational intellect. Even Hurtle Duffield and Elizabeth Hunter, complex, cultivated and intelligent as they are, operate from a much wider range of the mind than just the cogitating component; their agile but not always trustworthy minds sport and flicker across domains that the intellect eschews.

To complete the identification of the self in terms of the limited ego, people add what they have and what they do to what they think. The 'I' can then be reckoned up as the sum of social roles, possessions (amongst which are counted the possession of other human beings), achievements and activities. Having completed the reckoning, people then become frozen into their roles: Mr Bonner *is* his material prosperity, Amy is her family and lover, Basil Hunter is his acting, Boo is her parties. The stereotype may prove limiting, the character may long to repossess tracts of himself that have been amputated or buried, as Basil Hunter longs to become a whole human being and discover the as yet 'unplayed I' (ES p. 321), but often nothing short of an explosive and possibly mortal trauma will suffice to break the ice. In *The Cockatoos*, White shows several cases of good, honest, rational Australian couples, who are briefly and terrifyingly brought in contact with the voltage of the irrational which, because of their benumbed condition, they can only experience as diabolic or negative epiphanies. For others the 'cure' may be a self-conscious and painful struggle, as it is for Basil Hunter, while others again may have the curse gently removed, as Mr Feinstein is 'saved' by his moments of silent communion with Arthur Brown.

Although the central characters do, of course, tend to identify themselves partly in terms of thinking, doing or having, they all, in the end, have a strength at the centre which permits them to surrender these external adjuncts without being destroyed in their being. They can, finally, render up their personal identity for the sake of being identical with God. The self becomes the Self, atman becomes Atman, the Christ within is merged with Christ Pantocrator. Those who cannot render themselves up in this way prove the shallowness of the 'I' in which they believe.

The order that must be achieved within the psychic mandala cannot be imposed by external facets of the personality. The ego can never reach down into the centre, and its attempts to organize and dominate the personality frustrate the growth of the true self. It is by an open flow to and from the core of being that the divergent phenomena of mental life are ultimately given coherence. The potential self must emanate outward, for it is only by passing through a stage of fragmentation, confusion and multiplicity (the 'great splintering') that it can achieve its final unity. This end will be thwarted if, in the process of diversification, the 'I' chooses to believe in one of its external divisions at the expense of the totality.

One last quotation will highlight the significance of the discussion in this section:

> ... there is something I must find out about, which is neither marriage, nor position, nor the procedures of formal religion, nor possessions, nor love in *that* sense. If I could only ask Mother ... (ES p. 271)

THE BODY

The body, or outer circle of the mandala, has a very solid presence in White's novels. One of the most striking qualities of his books is the vivid, sometimes almost obsessive or hallucinated, concentration on the corporeal aspects of personality. He views human beings with an openness of vision, a freedom from conventional modes of perception, that often result in a concentration on details that are usually politely ignored. He sees gristle and sinews, veins in the eyeballs, tufts of hair, the texture and pores of skin, nostrils, knuckles and goitres. His subject is the Word made Flesh, and he creates a very vivid sense of the implications of 'being in the flesh'.

This very insistence on the body suggests, however, a profound ambivalence, both temperamental and metaphysical, in his attitude towards the flesh. There seems to be a fascinated revulsion in the books. Characters are drawn compulsively towards the flesh and at the same time desperately try to reject it. At a metaphysical level, this becomes the paradox that while the body is essential to the soul it is of less ultimate value; it is simultaneously the most and the least important of the soul's possessions.

The concentration on the uglier aspects of the body, and the choice of misshapen or ugly characters, may stem, at least at one level, from the belief that it is this aspect of the flesh, and not its perfection, that is the most apt emblem for the condition of the 'descended' soul. The body is not necessarily degraded, but involvement with it does make the soul vulnerable. That this vulnerability is feared, and that it must, at the same time, be accepted, is the root of the emotional ambiguity towards the body. White's attitude is encapsulated in a sequence from *The Living and the Dead*, in which Joe Barnett wills himself to look at a dead dog:

> The festoon of helpless guts torn out like the last existing privacy . . He made himself look . . . Man was born to this, no other dignity . . . But there was a dignity he was jealous of, his own body, his privacy of thought . . . (LD p. 257)

This same fascinated disgust for the more afflicted aspects of the body, coupled with a sense that there is a personal, an ethical and a spiritual duty to accept and embrace it, is found in many places in White. *Voss* opens with Laura Trevelyan caught in the dilemma, disgusted by the bodies of those around her (particularly the deformed Rose Portion) and aware that this disgust is a moral weakness:

> But Rose remained, her breasts moving in her brown dress. Laura Trevelyan had continued to feel repelled. It was the source of great unhappiness, because frequently she was also touched. She would try to keep her eyes averted, as she had from Jack Slipper. It is the bodies of these servants, she told herself in some hopelessness and disgust . . . am I a prig? So she wondered unhappily, and how she might correct her nature. (V p. 58)

The same temperamental ambivalence is felt in *The Vivisector*, in which Hurtle Duffield, through some necessity that he can scarcely articulate himself, is drawn time and again to create epiphanies of degradation. He is forced to paint Cutbush masturbating, Hero stabbing herself with a penis, the deformed Rhoda standing at a bidet or Nance spreadeagled on the floor. He seems determined to force into consciousness—his own and that of others—areas of bodily existence, or modes of incarnation, from which eyes are usually averted. Whether this is honesty or obsession is a question the novel leaves open.

This is not to say that White does not respond to physical beauty when it appears. He delights in creating portraits of beautiful women in gorgeous dresses, which he does with an evocative power equal to that of Lawrence or Proust. Limited as the temperaments of these women usually are, their beauty is a 'contribution to truth', and White does full justice to the poetry they create. This is particularly evident with Elizabeth Hunter, whose past beauty had something almost sacramental about it, even for the ascetic Mary de Santis. But physical beauty, in the last analysis, must be a spiritual limitation. If too much attention is concentrated on the outside of the mandala the inner circles will be ignored. Ugliness is not in itself a virtue, but those who possess it cannot take refuge on the surface, and must look for truth at deeper levels. From that truth, a new and more significant type of beauty will be radiated, as in the case of the conventionally 'plain' Laura Trevelyan, which supersedes the usual categories of beauty and ugliness. It is the beauty of Grace, not of form:

> Other individuals, of great longing but little daring, suspecting that the knowledge and strength of the headmistress might be accessible to them,

began to approach by degrees. Even her beauty was translated for them into terms they could understand. As the night poured in through the windows and the open doors, her eyes were overflowing with a love that might have appeared supernatural, if it had not been for the evidence of her earthly body: the slightly chapped skin of her neck, and the small hole in the finger of one glove, which, in her distraction and haste, she had forgotten to mend. (V p. 474)

The intimacy between the soul and the body, however, should not be underrated. It is not irrelevant to the self what kind of a body it is tied to. Except for the very deepest layer of personality, the characters' mode of 'being there' in the world will be determined by the form they assume, and the reactions of others to that form. None of White's characters are so intransigently strong or honest that they can withstand the conditioning effects of 'being' their bodies. Theodora is driven mad partly by the alienation from herself that occurs when she discovers how ugly she is. Rhoda Courtney has not only the body but also the personality of a hunchback. Everything about Mary Hare except her core of reality is shaped or misshaped by the destructive reactions of those around her, particularly her father, to her stunted body. Although being trapped in a plain, or even repellent, body may, as was suggested above, almost accidentally serve a higher spiritual end, White in no way romanticizes the existential suffering that it inflicts on the self, nor the degree to which the identification of the self is governed by it. He has a profound and sympathetic understanding of the subjectivity of his deformed or afflicted characters, and does not sentimentalize them from the outside.

As well as feeding into, and to a large extent shaping, the 'I', the body is also the medium through which this 'I' flows out into the world. Not only does it express the innate capacity for love or cruelty, for action or art, but also every part of the human body becomes a speaking symbol for emotional, moral or spiritual states. The body is the most important of the various language systems (which will be discussed further in Part Three) through which White gives expression to the flickerings of the inner life. Crutches tighten as emotions grow congested, hair evokes latent sexuality, heads shrink down to the bone in states of spiritual deprivation, lips swell or parch as emotions wax and wane, spiritual tension is expressed through a physical limp, breasts sidle, spectacles flash and teeth gnash and worry. To the same end—the expression of the inner life—the body is also coerced into taking on the nature of other forms of existence. There are as many metamorphoses in White as there are in Ovid. Bodies are frozen into the forms of architecture, sculpture, icons or wood-carving, then flow like water, music or fire. They take on the qualities of trees, flowers, scrub, sticks, stones, potatoes, birds, dogs or cows. They are like rock, wood, ash or air. On the purely descriptive level this constant flow of form and substance helps create that rich, bewildering density of texture that typifies White's writing. On the level of 'meaning', each change of state releases or identifies some condition of the soul.

The intimate, almost biological, link between the soul and the body, which has been stressed so often in this book, is expressed through many apparently obscene images in *The Vivisector* and *The Eye of the Storm*. These connect the physical processes of excretion or constipation, ejaculation or childbirth with central emotional, artistic or spiritual experiences. Even a cursory reading of *The Vivisector* reveals the more than metaphorical association of masturbation–fertilization and constipation–defecation with the different modes in which Hurtle Duffield experiences art. The same connection is revealed through the meanderings of the senile mind of the omnivorous Elizabeth Hunter, whose career in the 'hard, commodious world' comes to an end on her swan-bedecked commode, her soul being expelled like a last gaseous offering. This line of imagery culminates in the remarkable observation that 'souls have an anus' (ES p. 194). The import of this stream of cloacal symbolism is clear, if theologically unorthodox. The Word must, in every sense, be absorbed into and express itself through the flesh. Biology cannot be shirked.

At another extreme, the flesh and blood with which the Word is consubstantial can be seen as the bread and wine of Holy Communion. The mystery of man in Christ and Christ in man is brought home most fully in the symbolism of the Host. For White, the giving and receiving of Communion means always the generosity and acceptance of the questionable gift of carnality. To give of oneself without reservation, to be able to accept the passion and compassion—these are the marks of the true communicant. Mass may be celebrated in unexpected, even diabolical forms. The 'high old Mass' that Boyle of Jildra had predicted for Voss is celebrated by the reluctant communicant as a white grub is thrust into his mouth by his aboriginal captors. In the short story 'Sicilian Vespers', Ivy Simpson, rejecting her husband (the 'temporary host'), celebrates a Dionysiac communion with the flesh and blood of a chance American acquaintance. In *The Eye of the Storm*, Elizabeth Hunter's 'precious wafer of flesh' (ES p. 335) has always been denied to her children, her husband and even her lovers. At the moment of Grace in the centre of the cyclone, she is allowed—as she never has allowed herself—to offer the Host to the black, accepting swans. This symbolic act is followed through and consummated fifteen years later when, sensing that the only thing she now has to offer her children is her death, she voluntarily renders them this service. It is, perhaps, this last and first gift of herself, that requires the destruction of herself, which hallows Mrs Hunter. That her children are unworthy is irrelevant. If Christ had considered only the cannibalistic greed of His followers he might never have consented to be sundered and ingested. Mrs Hunter, who herself possesses a capacious maw, is no Christ, but the direction of this and the previous paragraph suggests how, in the depths and the heights, the destiny of the Word is bound up with the processes and the symbolism of the flesh.

I am not only my body, but only through my body can I know what I am. Yet having stressed this intimate link between soul and body, it is necessary to turn and point out that it is not complete identification. White, were we to give him a philosophic label, is an ontological, not a phenomenological existentialist. Although existence in the body predominates for much of the time, the core of being has a higher ontological reality. All things are real, but some are more real than others. This brings us to the metaphysical ambivalence which underlies the temperamental difficulties felt by so many of White's characters. The body is the only vehicle for, but the greatest burden to, the soul. The soul only takes on existence by wearing the clothes of flesh, yet as the core of being is raised to a higher level its bodily encumbrance becomes increasingly anachronistic. During the first phases of its cycle, the 'I' feels no disparity between itself and the body. But towards the end this congruity falls apart. One cannot say 'I am my body' but only, with decreasing relevance, 'I have a body'. As time goes on, the once organic relationship of body and soul turns into a rather uneasy coalition of core and carapace.

As the soul approaches its zenith, the body is seen at its most clumsy, afflicted or dilapidated. Stan Parker is last seen externally as a grouchy old man with a stick, Laura Trevelyan as a plain headmistress with a chapped neck and a cough, Mary Hare as a singed and repulsive animal and, of course, Elizabeth Hunter's already repulsive frame is tortured into ultimate monstrosity by the fiend's mask that Flora paints on her.

White's style, as well as his situations, emphasizes the dichotomy of aspiring soul and earth-bound body. Not less but more emphasis is placed on the incongruity of the flesh as the soul swims closest to the surface. White holds the husk in his tenderly ironic hands as the spark darts free. This concentration on the mundane, which occurs in every book as the soul is about to 'doff the outgrown garment of the body' (RC p. 480), creates a tension which prepares the reader for the final division. Any irony involved is intended for the flesh, not the soul; the more the grotesqueness of the body is emphasized, the less important it is felt to be. Every book ends with the implication that the shell has, or will, split apart, having outlived its protective and gestative functions.

6
The Social Mandala

THE FAMILY

This chapter employs the same mandalic structure as the previous one, but now the focus will be changed. The centre of the mandala-social is the individual, the Unique One, and the outer limit is society. Between the centre and the circumference of this new mandala intervenes the family. Family life is the first and most crucial encounter that the individual has as he emanates outwards into the human world. The destructive and creative potentials of the family knot have been impressively documented by psychoanalytical theorists over the last half century, and Patrick White's novels, taken at the purely psychological level, are rich and often horrifyingly accurate accounts of zones of experience that have been codified by such writers as Freud, Jung or R. D. Laing.

But the family is not simply a psycho-social phenomenon. It is also the arena in which many of the most crucial spiritual conflicts are fought out and resolved. The intimate link between the family and religion has been felt in all cultures and in every epoch. Greek myth and Wagnerian opera, Tibetan art and Egyptian fertility myths, Islamic schisms and Talmudic law can only be fully appreciated when we remember that Zeus, Wotan, Krishna, Osiris, Mohammed and Abraham were family men. The Greeks alone have left an impressive documentation of the murder, incest and depravity that is latent in the family. Christianity has enriched the concept of the family with its image of the sweetness and plenitude of the Holy Family and the agony and compassion of the Deposition. With its relish for paradox, Christianity has also gone even further than the Greeks in its celebration of Divine in-breeding by its re-telling of the Leda myth in which Mary appears simultaneously as daughter, spouse and mother of God. The more arcane areas of spiritual eroticism have found expression in Tibetan Buddhism, Kabbalism, alchemy and, closer to home, the lyrical celebration of incest in The Song of Solomon. A quotation from Gershom Scholem (whom readers interested in the background of the Chariot should also consult) illustrates the perennial importance of the latter aspect of family life:

It is well known that those deepest regions of human existence which are bound up with the sexual life play an important part in the history of mysticism. With few exceptions mystical literature abounds in erotic images. Even the mystical relation to God is frequently described as love between the soul and God, and Christian mysticism in particular has become notorious for the way in which it pushed this metaphor to extremes . . . the 'Songs of Songs' [is] a dialogue between God and the soul, i.e. an allegorical description of the path to the *unio mystica* . . .

. . . they [the Kabbalists] show no hesitation when it comes to describing the relation of God to Himself, in the world of the Sefiroth. The mystery of sex, as it appears to the Kabbalists, has a terribly deep significance. This mystery of human existence is for him nothing but a symbol of the love between the divine 'I' and the divine 'You', the Holy One, blessed be He and His Shekhinah.

For the rest [Kabbalism] rejected asceticism and continued to regard marriage not as a concession to the frailty of the flesh but as one of the most sacred mysteries. Every true marriage is a symbolical realization of the union of God and the Shekhinah.[15]

White weaves all the above elements into his portrait of the family which, like every aspect of his writing, is simultaneously psychological and metaphysical. The family is the central nexus of the various ethical and spiritual principles sketched in Part One. It is here that the negative abstractions of suffering, evil and hatred are clothed in personal forms. It is also here that the process of spiritual rebirth can take place. Behind all the individual and particular forms of suffering lies the primordial root of all suffering and evil—the original separation of the part from the whole. The painful moment of childbirth is the first act of cleavage and pain, through which the mystery of unity expresses itself. It is an agonizing time for the mother both physically and psychically. Being rent, she experiences the physical pain, the blood, which is the lot of Physis, and she also experiences the loss of organic unity with her child—a loss which may be at the root of her greed for possession in later life. It is, for the child, the first and worst trauma, for from this moment it is committed to its sheath of individual identity and painfully separated from half of its own hermaphroditic nature as well as from its original identification with the All. The family in its daemonic form is a fundamental act of violation, the cause of the schism which thrusts the soul into its destiny of painful particularity. After this original sundering the complexities and conflicts multiply as time unfolds until reconciliation and resolution seem impossible. But this unfolding process can be reversed if the will or grace to reverse it exists. The first marriage and the first birth can be redeemed by a second marriage and a second birth through which the individual can be infolded back into the mystery of unity from which it was cast by birth.

Certain personalities, emotions and situations recur sufficiently obsessively in the novels to suggest that they are the main components of what—without straying into the world of speculative biography—we may term 'the White family'. Three modes of this theoretical family can be distinguished which in the following discussion will be called 'the external family', 'the internal family' and 'the mythical family'. The argument will proceed from the first to the third of these levels of family life and, in doing so, will show how the daemonic aspects of the first two can be redeemed.

In keeping with the pattern of the mandala, the White individual finds himself embedded in a family of four. In all of the novels except *Riders in the Chariot*, 'the White family'—like the sociological family of Western society—is composed of father, mother and two children. Grandparents were components of the group in the early works, but as time passes their memory seems to fade. In four of the novels the children are brother and sister which may, perhaps, be regarded as the typical formation.

One of the children is beautiful, the other plain or ugly. One is often gifted, the other devoid of talent. One is sometimes possessed of a grace of spiritual origin, the other being earth-bound or worse. These qualities are distributed differently in the different novels as is the author's sympathy, which may go to one, to both or to neither, but they are obviously key components of White's family consciousness. One or both may be scarred by the imprint of false parental attitudes during the formative years. The daughter often experiences rejection (by the mother in the case of Theodora Goodman, by the father in the case of Mary Hare), while the son may be the victim of over-possessiveness. Their lives can be quite distinct and separate, or so close that they cannot at times be separated. Most typically, however, there is both a distance and a bond—a bond based on mutual awareness of complicity in family guilt. It tends to be the brother who wishes to ratify this bond, while the sister, though tacitly or briefly acknowledging it, prefers to remain aloof from the corruptness she suspects in her brother.

It is the children who are the experiencing centre of the White family which is usually chronicled, explicitly or implicitly, by the second generation. This does not mean that the parents are always the victims of child chauvinism. Their lives are imaginatively penetrated and acted out, sometimes with a sympathetic awareness that parents, too, can be victims of the failures of communication within the family. But the children's gaze, especially when directed towards the mother, is often rather baleful.

Where tenderness is expressed it is centred on the experience of the father, who tends to be a shadowy figure in family life, too innocent, decent or weak to counter-balance the dominance of the mother. His life and death remain on the periphery of his children's interest. They tend to have water-colour emotions for him which are positive rather than neutral but not emphatic. They have affection and re-spect—sometimes even a tinge of contempt—for his innocence. They also have a muted yearning for his goodness and a muted guilt that they have not known or loved him better—a guilt made complex by the fact that they do not feel guiltier. He is an isolated, sometimes rather sad figure, seared by his inability to break down the barriers between himself and his wife and children. He is typically associated with the pastoral life, and is more at home with nature or books than with human relationships. He dies years before his wife, often con-sumed with a nameless longing for something never experienced. His death may be a matter of complete indifference to his children, or it may be the central trauma of their lives. Usually it is a matter for passing grief, nostalgia or remorse in lives whose current is flowing too strongly in other directions to permit a long sojourn in the backwaters of mourning. His death clears the way for a protracted confrontation, sometimes melancholy, sometimes murderous, between the children and the mother.

It is certainly the mother who dominates the family group. White has wrestled with her, in one form or another, throughout his novelistic career. Both *The Living and the Dead* and *The Aunt's Story* begin with her death, an event which, some three decades later, becomes the central theme of *The Eye of the Storm*. In this latter novel, the knife which Theodora Goodman could not bring herself to use is at last driven home by Basil and Dorothy Hunter, although it is also only here that White has conceded to the mother the possibility of Grace.

The mother is a formidable opponent for such a lifetime's duel. She is intelligent and beautiful, full of élan and wit, intoxicating even to those most aware of her flaws. She is also dominating and selfish, simultaneously greedy and frigid, allowing to others no right of denial while denying herself constantly to those who need her most. She is portrayed at two stages in her career, first at the zenith of her beauty and power, second in protracted old age when the spiritual bankruptcy concealed by the dazzle is most evident. In the latter state, she is depicted with horrifying fidelity to the details of physical and moral decay. She is shown in different forms in different books. Sometimes it is her coldness and ruthlessness which are emphasized, as in *The Aunt's Story*, while sometimes the venom is withdrawn, and she is left only with her inability to love and her etiolated old age. Sometimes her attributes are distributed among several characters in the same novel. In *The Tree of Man*, Amy parker has her aspect as voracious mother and unfaithful wife, while Madeleine possesses her flair and her frigidity.

This woman is experienced as a despoiler and a quester, a betrayer and a creator of poetry. She is forced to violate innocence, for when it appears, as it does in her husband, his pastoral heritage or one of her children, it does so in a paucity of form that she cannot accept as an adequate vehicle for the type of intoxication she wishes to create. Her quest is more carnal than that of her husband, and she is sometimes forced by his self-enclosed goodness to commit actual or meta-phorical acts of adultery. Sympathy is almost always withdrawn from her, although understanding and admiration may remain. *The Eye of the Storm*, which gives the most complete portrait of her, is both an exception and a consummation. In writing this novel White seems finally to have pierced the heart of a lifetime's antagonist and found there an unsuspected grace. It may have been an act of exorcism, for in the next book, *The Cockatoos*, she has disappeared, and her place is taken by the elderly, childless couple who were a swelling sub-theme from *The Solid Mandala* on.

After this brief sketch of the external family, attention will now be turned to the internal or psychological family. In doing so, the names of Freud, Jung and R. D. Laing will be used, but this is only to indicate areas of interest. White's artistic understanding of the family is too deep and comprehensive to benefit from the rigid application of any psychoanalytical orthodoxy.

The first area of interest might be termed 'the Greek' (out of deference to Sophocles), 'the Elizabethan' (out of respect for the Tudor imbroglios of Webster and Shakespeare) or 'the Freudian' (after the man who first made manifest the latent incest and murder of the domestic hearth). The themes of murder and incest appear repeatedly in White's novels. Murder—particularly matricide—has been with him from the beginning, as suggested by the first pages of *The Living and the Dead* and *The Aunt's Story*, and by Theodora's instinct to pick up an actual knife to defend herself against her mother's metaphorical one. The incestuous component is more muted in the early novels, being limited to the feelings of daughter for father, as in the case of Ruth Godbold. With *The Solid Mandala*, however, it becomes and remains a more explicit part of characterization. The need to murder another member of the family may arise from a desire for freedom, from a sense of revenge or from the instinctive impulse, noted in Chapter Two, to make the innocent or the afflicted suffer.

Both the murderous and the incestuous urges can flow in many directions within the White family. The desire to kill can flow from daughter to mother (Theodora), from son to mother (Basil Hunter), or between siblings (Waldo Brown). Equally, the sexual impulse can flow from daughter to father (Mary de Santis), mother to son (Mrs Courtney), or, again, between siblings (Basil and Dorothy Hunter). But the key component of the classical Freudian approach—the son's desire to kill the father and sleep with the mother—seems absent. Admittedly, if the novels are viewed as wish-fulfilment fantasies, then the early death of the father and the long possession of the mother might seem significant. Or, again, we may find the Hamlet situation much in evidence: the death or 'murder' of the good or loved father, the adultery of the mother with the unworthy lover and a consequent spirit of revenge in the children. But Freud's system, even when helped out by 'displacement', 'ambivalence' and 'the censor', does not provide enough clues to solve the jig-saw. The current of antagonism that runs towards the mother seems genuine, as does the affection or compassion for the father. White's men are not seeking mother surrogates; one mother a lifetime seems sufficient. Although there is a spirit of revenge abroad, sometimes mixed with distaste for adultery, it does not seem to be generated by a suppressed sexual urge. The Oedipus complex is not a driving power in White's writing.

This is not to say that the mother does not have a profound impact upon the psyche of her children. As R. D. Laing has shown, there are more than Freudian currents flowing in the family, and it is more rewarding to turn to Laing than to Freud to understand the nature of the hostility between children and parents. The parents in White are themselves 'burnt ones', and false parental attitudes can set in motion in the children processes of self-alienation which, if unchecked, can deepen from frigidity into neurosis and from neurosis into psychosis or hell. The case history of Theodora Goodman has already been examined, and shown to be a study of schizophrenia induced by ontological insecurity for which the mother was chiefly to blame. The estrangement of the children from the outside world, their inability to form genuine human attachments, their emotional coldness, their substitution of great ideas, great vocations, social ambition or (in the case of Ray Parker) petty seduction and petty crime for meaningful relationships—stem from an alienation from themselves that is largely the fault of their parents. The crime of the mother is not her adulteries, the obsession with the mother is not sexual. The children have a hole in the centre where the core should be, and feel a bitter resentment against the mother for causing the original rift of the self from the self, which perhaps only intercession or Grace can heal.

Jung, the third of the theorists mentioned above, helps pinpoint another important area of psychic life in which the family plays a role. As noted in the last chapter, through the twin processes of projection and internalization, psychic components are thrown out and associated with figures in the environment, or else such figures are brought in and transformed into symbols of some aspect of the temperament. This happens particularly between members of the family, where the sister or mother may become the personification of the *anima*, the brother or father may become the personification of the *animus*. The autonomous power of these psychic allegories has already been seen in the case of Waldo Brown, whose mother gives a face to an archetypal element of his nature which has been repressed most of his life, and in the case of Theodora who 'cures' herself by personifying the male component of her double nature as Holstius—the *avatar* of Father. With the introduction of the idea of the Jungian archetypes, we have now reached the border between the inner, psychological family and the mythical family. If the family knot is to be untied, it will be by taking the step into this third domain.

The various elements of the external and internal families that have been discussed above—father's goodness, weakness and early death, mother's destructiveness and her adultery, the inchoate bond between brother and sister, the murderous and sexual impulses, the alienation from the self and the appearance of archetypal figures from the unconscious—will now be woven into a more complete pattern of which the central theme will be the quest for unity.

In many places in White there is an explicit or implicit merging of the individual father and son with the Father and Son of the Trinity, e.g.: ' "To our Father," the mystic word troubled her more than when it cropped up in her prayers.' (ES p. 474); '. . . Basil my Beloved Only Son' (ES p. 415). Father can be seen as Adam, turned out of Paradise for the sins of his wife, or as the wounded King whose heritage has become the Wasteland. In another aspect he is a primordial God, seen only in His aspect of goodness, which is often identical with impotence. His wound is both his ineffectiveness and also the knife thrust that the Queen inflicts upon him. He remains unactivated by contact with Physis, but is vulnerable to her stabs. His death leaves the Son alone to confront the wicked Queen or Eve–Physis, in a wasteland which is now presided over not by the mild benevolent God but by a usurping demiurge—The Vivisector. The Son inherits the Wound of the Father in a lethal form, since his experience in the fallen world goes deeper. The affliction of the first Adam becomes the wounds of the second Adam or Christ which, paradoxically, can only be cured by a deeper involvement with the principle of Eve-Physis. He must overcome this aspect of the Eternal Female, and must reinstate and sanctify the violated marriage of the Father by marriage with the True Bride. If he succeeds, the wounds will be cured, the Garden will bloom again, and the evil demiurge will be replaced by the Grace that emanates from the true, the Hidden God.

The inheritance of the father's spiritual wound in an aggravated form appears explicitly in *The Solid Mandala* and *The Eye of the Storm*. In the former, both Waldo and Arthur identify at moments with the limp of their apostate father. Waldo, terrified of the idea of 'wounds', rejects the association but Arthur can accept his affliction, acknowledge the suffering of Christ, and is, therefore, 'cured of all'. Sir Basil Hunter's affected limp becomes something more serious during his visit to 'Kudjeri' where he first cuts himself at the dam (ES p. 493), and then when he thrusts his foot into the boot of his dead father (the 'deposed monarch', ES p. 505) and can only with difficulty remove the 'deformity'. His sister—for whom the Wasteland is Australia itself—does manage to yank the boot off and relieve her brother of the limp it inflicted (ES p. 509), but of course this is no real solution to the inherited wound. For he who wishes to make himself King—and this is the explicit goal of at least Voss and Basil—the wounds must be accepted, the affliction must be acknowledged. This is the painful truth that Mrs Volkov thrusts on Hurtle Duffield when she writes to him and says that it is he, not Rhoda, who is the afflicted one.

The greatest wound of all is the divorce within the self. This divorce can take many forms, but its ultimate cause or symbol is the betrayal of the old Adam by the old Eve—the rift between Nous and Physis. This divorce must be redeemed by the second marriage, the marriage of the Son with the Bride, which is also the symbolic conjunction of brother with sister. This truth is revealed to Arthur Brown during his reading of old books: '. . . there is therefore nothing better or more

venerable than the conjunction of myself with my brother'. It is also
to be found in The Song of Solomon: 'You have ravished my heart,
my sister, my bride, . . .' (4:9); 'O that you were like a brother to me,
that nursed at my mother's breast!' (8:1). It is important to stress that
the White psychic family has two, not one, female components. This is
made clear in *The Ham Funeral* where, at the lower level, we find
Eve–Physis, and at the upper level we find the Sister–Bride. The son's
mission is to confront and possibly overcome the former and to wed
the latter. This marriage restores to its original integrity the divided
hermaphrodite, who comes together like the two parts of a double-
yolked egg and, in doing so, destroys the power of Physis who was
responsible for the original sundering. It is only now that the wounds
of the Son begin to be healed by the ministrations of the loving Bride.
We find the most mystical, and also the most beautiful celebrations of
this marriage in *Voss* and *Riders in the Chariot*:

While the woman sat looking down at her knees, the greyish skin was slowly
revived, until her full, white, immaculate body became the shining source of
all light.
By its radiance, he did finally recognise her face, and would have gone to
her, if it had been possible, but it was not; his body was worn out.
Instead, she came to him, and at once he was flooded with light and
memory. As she lay beside him, his boyhood slipped from him in a rustling of
water and a rough towel. A steady summer had possessed them. Leaves were in
her lips, that he bit off, and from her breasts the full, silky, milky buds . . .
So they were growing together, and loving. No sore was so scrofulous on his
body that she would not touch it with her kindness. He would kiss her wounds,
even the deepest ones, that he had inflicted himself and left to suppurate. (V
pp. 417–18)

Again, he was the Man Kadmon, descending from the Tree of Light to take the
Bride. Trembling with white, holding the cup in her chapped hands, she ad-
vanced to stand beneath the *Chuppah* . . . This, explained the cousins and
aunts, is at last the *Shecchinah*, whom you have carried all these years under
your left breast. As he received her, she bent and kissed the wound in his hand.
(RC p. 483)

This marriage cannot cure all the wounds, as it still is bound by
temporal necessity, and Time itself is a wound that bleeds. But it is the
last necessary step before the final *unio mystica* between the soul and
God. This is the moment of rebirth which reverses the direction of the
first birth, being an infolding, not an unfolding. Only now can the
deepest Wound be healed, and the Son enter His rightful heritage.
The hero's mission is singularly lacking in sexual urgency,

whatever other daemons may be driving him. The same cannot be said of the female members of the family for whom carnality is the chief vehicle for the spirit. Eve–Mary is seeking a Lord that she can worship and a Son that she can bear. She finds herself caught in a knot in which Father, Husband, Lover and Son can change places and be substituted one for another. This tangle has been exploited by Freud, but it was first experienced by the Virgin Mary, who betrayed her worthy husband with a lover who was also her father and her son. Guilt and bewilderment are generated by the complexities of such a situation. But behind the carnal drive lies a quest for Grace and Illumination that are provided by the Holy Spirit, as is suggested by Nance Lightfoot:

'Sometimes the birds flew so low I could feel the noise of their wings and got the idea my head might be split open and would swallow up one of those white birds then when the wound had closed I would see things as they're supposed to be . . .' (Viv p. 255)

As Eve–Physis, the woman is tempted to transgress the law and eat the forbidden fruit. As Mary, she is often frustrated by the miscarriage or loss (metaphorical or literal) of her Son. The pain and bleeding of childbirth are her point of contact with the sufferings of Christ, the point where agony and loss become personal. All these ingredients are present in 'Sicilian Vespers' in which the 'rational' Ivy Simpson has a negative epiphany or moment of Dionysiac communion with an American father-surrogate during vespers in San Fabrizio. The passage is quoted at length as it is the most complete and concentrated expression of the drive behind the adulteries of so many other White women:

. . . their progress was crabwise.
'. . . if we could take a proper look—which we can't, all considered—we'd find a very beautiful Passion.'
(Oh the Passion frightening word the tears of blood you have never shed stillborn is not a real one not a dead husband either in that incredible event you might bow your head along with the dust-coloured gentlewomen . . . and learn from nuns how to climb a ladder of prayer.)
'. . . but the most magnificent of all, Ivy, is the Pantocrator.'
This was not why she had come to San Fabrizio with Clark Shacklock, the commonplace, perspiring American. She would not look at the Pantocrator. She would rather shut her eyes tight, close her mind to intellectual duplicity. Or discover her own, vulgar, fleshly self.

It was herself, however, clawing at Clark as though his solid bulk might save. Under the Pantocrator's eye. Surrounded by the scraggy saints.

She could have vomited over the brown tripe the two of them were preparing to hang from ancient rust-eaten nails in the glass *duomo*, but instead she was dragging Him (her Lover) into this obscure side chapel . . . (C pp. 239–40)

'When do they communicate?' she asked with fearful hope.

'Never communion at vespers!' Clark Shacklock spoke with authority.

She was convinced he was the RC she had suspected; so she was committing the triple blasphemy: against her honest husband, their enlightenment, and most grievously, their love for each other.

Now only Aubrey Tyndall was laughing: the sensual man who had never recognized her in his lifetime, but whom she had nourished inside her for all of hers.

All that was happening should have been enough, but she visualized the nuns' greed as the pitiful wafer collapsed in their mouths, and regretted her lost opportunity to blaspheme in addition against the Holy Ghost.

At dust level . . . they were lunging together, snout bruising snout . . . She wrapped herself around him . . . while the enormous tear swelled to overflowing in the glass eye focused on them from the golden dome.
. . . I can see inside the box in which He my Dearly Beloved Husband has thrown off the sheet is rising from amongst the limp grey wrinkles on the yellow bed offering Himself afresh for sacrifice under the extinct acrylic object. (C pp. 242–3)

The woman's solution, if it can be found, is complementary to that of the man—she becomes the Bride and the Mother. She is celebrated in the former aspect as Dulcie Saporta at the end of *The Solid Mandala*, in the latter as Ruth Godbold in Alf Dubbo's 'Deposition'. Mrs Poulter combines both qualities as she and Arthur complete and fulfil one another. Often this moment of discovery or acknowledgement coincides with the moment of loss. The Lord reveals and withdraws Himself at the same time, leaving the Bride a widow, Mary weeping at the foot of the Cross. Thus we find Rhoda Courtney acknowledging Hurtle as her Dear Lord as he dies, or Mary Hare finding and losing Christ in Himmelfarb. Several of the stories in *The Cockatoos* end on this bereaved note.

The condition of the bereaved woman is particularly in evidence in

the novels up to and including *Voss*. We find her as the nun-figures of
Alys Browne, Eden Standish, Theodora Goodman and Laura
Trevelyan. This angular and uncompromising figure spends much of
her life alone, having lost her flesh-and-blood Lord early. But she
carries his image within, just as Himmelfarb or Arthur carry their
Brides within. This is most evident in the case of Theodora and
Holstius. Unlike the later heroines, she tends to have a rather
critical attitude to the men in her life; Laura, as has been pointed out,
is as harsh on Voss as Beatrice is on Dante, and for the same end. This
nun-figure disappears mysteriously after *Voss*, leaving the males in a
slightly stronger position within the later books.

Although the marriage, for the woman, is brief, and the depth and
duration of deprivation is formidable, the fact that the union has
been made leads her just as inevitably as her male counterpart
towards the final Marriage with the Christ Pantocrator against Whom
Ivy Simpson blasphemes and for Whom she longs.

One last but important member of the White family has been
reserved for the coda of this section. The most striking biological and
psychological condition in White's novels is that of childlessness.
Happy Valley begins with a miscarriage, *The Cockatoos* is devoted to the
condition of childless couples, and between these two there is a long
list of characters who are frustrated in their maternal instincts (which
are not just limited to women). This recurrent sense of barrenness or
loss seems to be an enduring component of the temperament of the
author. As though to compensate for his sense of emptiness, a 'spirit
child' appears in several of White's novels who fills the gap left by
biological sterility. She appears as both Lou Parrott and Katina
Pavlou in *The Aunt's Story*, as Mercy in *Voss* and as Kathy Volkov and
the little psychopomp in *The Vivisector*. The temptation to allegorize
her is strong, especially in *Voss* where some readers have accused Mercy of being an unnecessary piece of symbolic lumber. I would prefer
to regard her as a touching and anomalous sport of pure creation,
born of emotional not thematic need. At the end of this highly
schematized section I will content myself with merely pointing to her
existence and then leave her—as Hurtle is forced to do—to weave the
pattern of her own life outside the domain of authorial omniscience.

SOCIETY

As the body is to the core of being, so society in general is to the
unique individual. This relationship is expressed through a typical
nodal pattern that appears at moments of emotional or spiritual in-

tensity in the novels. An individual at the centre undergoes a supreme moment of exhilaration or despair. From this central character circles of awareness radiate out, through one or two who are intimately involved in the experience, to others who are less intimately concerned but still have some intuition of the significance of the mystery, to a periphery that swirls about, sometimes indifferent, sometimes repelled, sometimes fascinated, sometimes concentrated on the centre with murderous hatred. As with the body, White presents 'society'—the mass of humanity at the circumference—vividly and concretely, drawing its lineaments and imitating its gestures with the accuracy of a true novelist of manners; as with the body, however, in spite of, or even because of its apparent substantiality, society exists at a lower ontological level than the Unique One.

Examples of this mandalic relationship between the Unique One and the herd occur repeatedly. In *The Aunt's Story*, Theodora suddenly blazes up at a dance, sweeping Frank Parrott for a moment into the vortex of her exhilaration. Fanny has a brief awareness, half-impressed, half-repelled, of what is happening, while outside these figures the ritual of the dance carries on. As Mrs O'Dowd, in *The Tree of Man*, dies, she is surrounded by an obtuse and shallow chorus of relatives, neighbours and gossips. Only Amy Parker is able to enter a little way into the mystery of death with her friend.

In *Voss*, this same type of situation gathers around Laura, whom we see in almost every chapter at the centre of such a circle. At the leave-taking, she experiences agonies of involvement and apprehension of which only Palfreyman is aware; at the ball, in the middle of her ordeal, she is tortured by rivers of subterranean suffering which Dr Badgery intuits, and Tom glimpses briefly, but which go unnoticed by the social rout. At the party in the last chapter, Laura once more sits at the centre of intensity, surrounded by an inner circle of initiates, drawing the passing attention of others, while being the target for malicious gossip for those on the outside.

In *The Eye of the Storm*, there are wheels within wheels, Elizabeth Hunter being in the centre of a public mandala in the present and a private mandala of memory. In the former, it is her nurses and housekeeper who sense the mystery she represents, while it is the children who, repressing their longings, converge on her with the brutality of their murderous social intentions. The symbolic configuration is highlighted by the use of terms such as 'idol', 'goddess', 'relic', 'shrine' or 'oracle' for Mrs Hunter, and 'priestess', 'votary' or 'acolyte' for the inner circle of attendant women. These images are not unironical, as the 'old mummy' has much that is pagan or corrupt

in her nature, but the brief bursts of illumination that flash from the
hieratic centre and are felt by all who come in contact with her,
suggest that the authorial irony is tempered by recognition of the
mystery that the old lady, almost in spite of herself, is the custodian of.
The two circles fuse together at the moment when the children drive
the knife home, which is also the moment when, for the first time, Mrs
Hunter allows herself to return in memory to Brumby Island and live
again the experience of the Eye.

The symbolic configuration suggested above points inevitably to
the central dramatic episode of the Christ story. In *Voss* and *Riders in
the Chariot*, this implicit parallel is made manifest. The heart of the
mystery that Voss, Palfreyman and Himmelfarb enter is linked
explicitly with the Crucifixion, and in the latter novel, the characters
who surround Himmelfarb find themselves compulsively adopting
the archetypal roles of those who created the original Christian mandala. This subject will be returned to later in the section.

When we speak of 'society' in White's novels, we usually mean the
hierarchical class-status system with its accompanying rites,
ceremonies, icons and conventions. These he imitates and parodies
brilliantly at every level from the 'old family' down to the flotsam of
the sub-proletariat, catching the typical clothes and houses, gestures
and speech patterns, occupations and interests of each. He shows how
social class can dominate the individual, from the typical flowers that
each will plant to the typical modes of sensibility or temperament that
each will generate. He is partisan for no particular class, although
there is something of the aristocrat and the peasant about him. The
cultivated and 'amusing' conversation of the society lady is no more
'real' than the mateship and booze of the workers. The exquisite sensibility of a Boo Davenport and the banal aspirations of a Nance
Lightfoot exist at the same level. White is interested in the life of the
temperament and of the spirit. To the extent that the individual
allows himself to be dominated by, or to define himself in terms of the
conventions of any class, he is limiting and falsifying his inner life.
White caricatures those who have become model representatives of a
class because they have already caricatured themselves, subordinating
their painful individuality to the outward forms of conformity.

The 'social' characters are rendered impotent in White by a double
focus of style. White observes their social behaviour with the eye of
a satirist and their inner lives with the eye of a religious philosopher.
Characters like Mr Bonner, Mrs Standish, Dorothy Hunter or Frank
Parrott are created (or imitated), analysed and satirized in the one
simultaneous creative act. He takes their souls seriously but ridicules

their antics, for it is their antics that trivialize their spiritual potential. From the moment they come into being in his pages they lack dramatic autonomy; the analyst and satirist will not allow them that opacity which creates an illusion of freedom. They have little chance of offering resistance to their creator, who knows them too well. From mild Austenian irony, through Dickensian caricature to Swiftian ferocity and beyond that to heights of prophetic denunciation, his style probes and undermines any pretensions to autonomy they might have. In doing so, of course, he violates one of the major canons of twentieth-century critical orthodoxy. Great artists seldom feel obliged to allow themselves to be confined by academic dogmatism.

A certain irony, aimed at the 'endorsed' characters, has been remarked elsewhere in this book, an irony that becomes increasingly wry as the climax approaches. The satire aimed at the minor, social characters stems from the same metaphysical source but has an opposite import. Both are generated by an awareness of the discrepancy between the centre and the circumference. In the first case, White is expressing the discrepancy between the wine of the soul and the battered chalice into which it is poured. In the second case, his satire expresses the opposite incongruity: the splendour of the vessel (money, status, looks, self-confidence) and the insipidity of the liquid it contains. The satirist and the visionary are both working to the same end, and the denunciations always serve the vision.

But many of the characters—major and minor—whose spiritual predicament White investigates are not actually frozen into one class or one culture. They are caught in the tension of two class, cultural or religious loyalties. In such a dilemma, the soul cannot sink into a cozy stereotype. Beneath surface conformity there lies a psychic confusion which lays the soul open to the analytical eye, whose knife may operate more bluntly on the pure conformist. The conflict in the mind of the déclassé aristocrat, the new-rich merchant, the immigrant or the apostate reveals the fundamental principles of personality better than does the assurance of their less troubled neighbours. The personality splitting noted in the last chapter is very often the result of the importunate and contradictory demands of two cultural cross-currents. Within the fixed social categories of the Australian class system there is a great deal of individual mobility, and it is often these mobile individuals whom White selects to highlight the emotional and spiritual malaise that underlies the facade of normality. The list of those who have abandoned their shameful or painful roots in order to erect a new and more acceptable persona is almost endless. Mrs Standish is the first full-length portrait, and the line continues through the motley crowd of poseurs at the Hôtel du Midi, the ersatz career of Thelma Forsdyke, the perilous material prosperity of the Bonners, the agonies of the apostates Rosetree, Feinstein and George Brown to the brief sketch of the newly 'arrived' Mrs Trotter in *The Vivisector*. The various layers of the synthetic soul are encapsulated with biting comedy in the case of Dorothy Hunter; the misfortune of Dorothy, la Princesse de Lascabanes, is to feel her most French in Australia, her most Australian in France: '"*O Mon Dieu, aidez-moi!*" she gasped, before assuming another of her selves, or voices, to utter, "Mother!" and lower, "Mum!"' (ES p. 46)

The same observation applies to the 'outsiders' who serve White as heroes and heroines. At a social level many of these are 'different' because they bring to their context a different set of assumptions, a different way of looking at the world from their parochial Australian neighbours. *Voss* deals with a society in which in one sense everybody is an 'outsider' since all have first-hand memories of other countries and other climates. But Voss is particularly alien by virtue of his strange Germanic ways and outlook. Himmelfarb, Dubbo and even Ruth Godbold bring to white middle-class anglican Australian society the legacy of a totally different culture and way of life. Arthur and Waldo Brown start off with an initial sense of being different from the Australian kids at their school, while Hurtle Duffield finds it difficult to 'pass' at any level of society, since he is gifted or cursed with two class identities rather than one.

One should not emphasize this aspect of White's major characters too heavily, however. Although many of them are, or become, social outsiders, and many are outsiders through the oddity of their minds or ugliness of their appearance, this is only tangentially related to the existence of the Grace that marks them off from others. Being an outsider, either by culture or by virtue of some personal affliction, is neither necessary nor sufficient to generate the true selfhood which should be the basis of character.

Though some kind of dislocation from socially defined normality helps activate the core of being, it is not necessary. Some characters—in particular Theodora Goodman, Laura Trevelyan, Hurtle Duffield and Elizabeth Hunter—are born or adopted into a clearly defined social group in which, had they been prepared to compromise, they could easily have passed and been accepted. Indeed in the case of Elizabeth Hunter, the nonconformity is invisible to the eye of the beholder and she appears at home in, even mistress of, the world of social normality. Then again although some characters, like Voss, can release their daemon only by escaping from their community, others, like Dulcie Feinstein, find themselves by rejoining their rejected culture. Others again, like Stan Parker, live contentedly inside their community all their lives, without necessarily falsifying themselves. Above all, most of the major characters are not Unique Ones—*zaddikim*, explorers, artists or saints—because they are social outsiders, but are outsiders because of their destiny. Voss leaves his community because of his daemon, Laura cannot accept hers because of her 'vocation'. Himmelfarb does not acquire Messianic delusions as a 'reffo' Jew in Australia but as a respected professor and pillar of his community in Germany; he actually comes to Australia because his mission of atonement will not let him merge with the secular society of the Promised Land. Hurtle Duffield, though afflicted with cultural schizophrenia, is basically estranged from both his lower- and his upper-class contexts by his secret gift. It is the vocation that causes the estrangement and not, as Freud might have it, the other way around.

Furthermore, social estrangement is not sufficient to generate the inner Grace. There are many characters in White who cannot conform to their social environment, are deformed, afflicted or beyond the social pale, who are destroyed or degraded, not uplifted, by their experience. Harry Rosetree is driven to suicide by his conflict of loyalties. The characters at Khalil's brothel are as much outside conventional society as Ruth Godbold is, or more so, but do not possess her inner light. Palfreyman's sister is emotionally crushed by her humped back.

Being 'different', then, although it may be a useful spiritual irritant or catalyst, is neither necessary nor sufficient to produce the Unique One. At most, one can say that where the individual is strong enough to sustain the estrangement, it prevents the soul from taking the easy way out, prevents it using conformity as a bolt-hole from inner reality, which it would be only human to use if it were available.

Although the Unique One lives apart from society and at a higher level of being, there is still a necessary relationship that exists between him and the outer rim of the mandala, a relationship which is analogous to that between the self and the body. The same fascinated revulsion, the same sense of necessary involvement and temperamental aversion that exists between soul and body is found in the relationship of the special individual and the mass of humanity. He is impelled, sometimes by will, sometimes by inclination, to embrace the body of corporate humanity. He is fearful of the ravages and indignities that this involvement will inflict upon him. Elyot Standish, blocking his ears to the sounds of the feared and longed-for streets, and Hurtle Duffield, shut up in his attic but peering out at passers-by, manifest the same symptoms. Life in the streets is banal, vulgar, irreverent and distasteful, but it is life. And those who live also create. It is an ethical duty for the saint, an aesthetic necessity for the artist and a spiritual duty for every man to descend to the condition of common humanity. But the very insistence that White places on this necessity suggests a temperament divided against itself on the subject.

We see characters carrying out this act of descent in many places. Both *The Living and the Dead* and *The Ham Funeral* end with an acceptance of, and merging into, the life of the streets. Laura Trevelyan wills herself to embrace Rose, and thereby all humble folk. Mordecai Himmelfarb, by learning to accept the warm, sickly body of Israel the dyer, learns also to accept the hitherto repellent association with collective Jewry. Arthur Brown finds less difficulty than earlier characters in immersing himself in the life of the streets, celebrating the ends of wars or talking with strangers in trains and buses. Hurtle Duffield plunges himself into the city after his stroke as into renewing or baptismal water, gaining new life from its banal vigour. In these two novels, there is a softening of attitude towards life in the city, a more relaxed flow into humanity; what for Elyot Standish was almost impossible to achieve occurs spontaneously and without strain in the cases of Arthur and Hurtle. This change corresponds in time with the author's move from Castle Hill to Centennial Park, where much of the recent writing has been set.

Along with this necessary and voluntary descent is a fear of being 'given over' to the mob. Just as the soul may become the victim of the body, so the unique individual can find himself powerless and persecuted amongst those he had felt it was his duty to love. Theodora Goodman is led away by the Johnsons to be put in a mental hospital, just as Arthur Brown is led off by the police sergeant to a similar destination. As Stan Parker's strength fails him, the outward circumstances of his life are increasingly dictated by others. Hurtle Duffield, with an irony typical of the malicious God in whom he believes, is laid low on the pavement outside the very shop he would have liked most to avoid—that of Cutbush. In *Voss*, the King is deposed and executed by those of his 'subjects' he has loved most. Elizabeth Hunter finds herself at the 'mercy' of her children. In *Riders in the Chariot*, the latent Christianity of this situation is made overt in Himmelfarb's crucifixion.

The Christian parallels suggest both the limitation and the function of the power invested in the 'crucifiers' on these occasions. Although the central character is given over, his special destiny or core of being remains untouched. Theodora's black rose continues to lead a life of its own, Hurtle paints his greatest paintings when he is most dependent on others, and Elizabeth Hunter is not forced to surrender anything which she is not prepared to render voluntarily. Himmelfarb is fulfilled, rather than destroyed, by the murderous practical joke at Rosetree's. Even when it appears to possess most power over the individual, society succeeds only in serving a higher end.

When reading Patrick White's novels, we get a sense of a temperament moving among the members of 'normal' society like an anthropologist living with an alien tribe. His perception and description of the rites and ceremonies, icons and folk-ways are extraordinarily accurate and vivid. Going below the surface, using evidence drawn partly from observation, partly from introspection, he penetrates, interprets and illuminates the secret springs of their nature, of which they would often themselves be unconscious. His alien frame of reference allows him to see things they cannot see, although those of the tribe who read his journals may equally feel that they have not been interpreted, but have been translated into a foreign language. Ultimately, one feels, he leaves the tribe and goes back to his own land from which he looks back on a country that has the vividness but also the evanescence of a dream.

PART THREE

THE NATURAL WORLD

7

Alternative Languages

White's characters have a living, organic relationship with the sensuous world that surrounds them. There is a sense of 'being there' in the phenomenal world, an openness to the pulsations and emanations of places and things which is more commonly found in poetry than in the novel. The major characters have a wider range of consciousness than most, which allows them to experience their environment in ways unknown to those who see the world only in terms of possession or utility, of having or doing. This sensitivity is one of the most remarkable qualities of White's writing, and is also an essential part of its meaning. Dialogue with the things of the material world is a means to, and a proof of, election.

The intensity with which the world is experienced suggests two analogies. First, it suggests the mode of life typical of the primitive, tribal, auguristic world. There seems to be an almost totemic or magical bond between man and nature. The flight of birds or movement of ants are portents, dreams are prophetic, rings and precious stones have a magical, talismanic power, sun and moon swing close to man and govern his life. In many ways, White's characters live in the world as man must have done in ancient China, Babylon or the heart of Australia before he civilized himself out of this immediacy of contact.

Secondly, an analogy is suggested with the increase in awareness which is produced by certain drugs, in particular by mescalin. As with the mescalin experience, White's characters become aware of objects in their surroundings which are usually ignored in the pursuit of habitual ends. Chairs and tables, leaves and scrolls of bark, pores of skin and the movements of hands suddenly take on an intensity uncharacteristic of normal modes of perception.

These analogies highlight tendencies in White's world-view but should not be pushed too far. The drug experience, though intense, is 'meaningless', pointing in any direction, and ultimately perhaps pointing only to itself. White is concerned not with experience for its own sake but with experience as it relates to meaning. And the totemic or auguristic world of pre-religion, though it does possess meaning, does so in an inflexible and external way. The sacramental union with nature is organized into static ritual, aimed ultimately at power over, rather than relationship with, nature. The mystery of omens can be decoded according to some system, the talismanic power of objects works independently of man, portents and signs point to an external fatality. Morality and religion are externalized, do not emanate from the soul, and the world is devoid of Grace.

The meaning with which White is concerned is the spiritual and ethical meaning of the inner life. We cannot approach his imagery externally; a study of the iconographic sources of his symbols, or an excessive insistence on the allegorical structure of the books, will obscure, rather than elucidate, his message. The images must be approached freely and flexibly, understood in terms of the total meaning of the book and the immediate circumstances of the characters at a particular stage in their emotional and spiritual development. The image patterns in White are an essential part of what he is communicating. They are alternative forms of language, working in conjunction with action, characterization, articulate utterances and mute intuitions to one end, the unfolding of the one vision. White applies himself to the difficult task of releasing the mute areas of experience that exist above and below the level of consciousness of characters in whose lives discursive thought and introspection play only a limited role. He uses all the resources of the sensuous world to this end, as different vocabularies through which to express the flickerings of the temperament and the progress of the soul.

In order to reveal and at the same time control the manifold and complex ways in which White uses images, a loose five-level system of exegesis will be employed. It has already been pointed out how the emotional, moral and spiritual are indissolubly tied together, and to attempt to interpret his images in only one dimension would not do justice to the density of the writing. The various levels of meaning do not contradict or undermine one another, but work simultaneously to explore a single experience from different points of view. The five components, set out as a paradigm, are as follows:

1. The Literal Level. At this level, things are simply themselves; it is the only level which would concern us if White were only a realist novelist. At this level, a marble is only a marble, not a cosmic mandala, a sunset is only a sunset, not a fiery chariot. This is the anchor

and the ground for the other levels, without which they could not exist. But granted this, and granted also that White's superb powers of description and evocation are amongst the highest attributes of his genius, little will be said about this level. Participating in a realm of pure existence, things on this plane do not 'mean' but 'are', and since the subject of this book is 'meaning', this first level will be taken for granted, and the remaining four will be concentrated on.

2. The Level of the Individual Situation or Objective Correlative. Every aspect of the material world, from parts of the human body to the cycle of the seasons, can be understood to express some nuance of mood or thought of the individual. There is a constant bond or sympathy between the temperament and the phenomenal world and to understand completely the full range of the emotional life one must be alive to that which is mirrored in nature.

3. The Level of the Human Condition. At this level, images portray, not the private inner world, but the general human condition under the gaze of eternity. This viewpoint tends to emerge as characters pass from youth to maturity, and accounts for a certain wryness of tone, a certain detachment from and irony towards even the most endorsed characters.

4. The Archetypal or Mythical Level. From the feet of the particular images grow the vast shadows of their archetypal counterparts. As we step back from the canvas, the bewildering profusion of the idiosyncratic and the prolixity of surface detail are resolved into the massive simplicity of mythic patterns. Their emergence continues the movement towards abstraction and generality already evident at Level 3, but this does not destroy the integrity of the first two levels, which are the domain of the particular. Rather, all four levels work together to release the fifth in which the unique and the universal merge.

5. The Numinous or Anagogical Level. This is where the mystery at which the other levels hint comes closest to the surface—this is the level of Grace. It resolves and justifies everything else, although its very intensity threatens to eliminate the sensuous content of the other levels. Here the soul is released, momentarily or permanently, from the body, as it achieves contact with the One which is the goal of its journey.

All of these levels exist in all the books, although the proportions vary. In *The Aunt's Story*, which is primarily a psychological study, it is the first two levels of imagery—the literal and the objective correlative—which predominate, whereas in *Riders in the Chariot* the emphasis on archetype and myth is so strong that at times it almost swamps considerations of convincing psychological motivation.

The system would not be complete if it were not pointed out that the principle of antinomy applies as much in the realm of imagery as it does in that of ideas. No image in itself is inherently 'good' or inherently 'bad'. At each level the image can be 'daemonic' or 'apocalyptic'[16]—an adjunct of destruction or redemption—according to its place in the action or the inner state of the actor. No understanding of White's imagery is possible without an acceptance of this basic ambivalence.

Imagery is an essential structural component of White's novels. Few of them have an external plot in the conventional sense, and their architectural firmness is provided to a large extent by the continuity, recurrence or counterpointing of key *leitmotifs*. The images are not frozen or static. They reappear throughout the course of the action, binding it together and directing it. The themes are unrolled through the development and accretions of the images, and to understand the significance of these images we must take into account their dynamic as well as their static functions. Although every level can appear at any point in the books, there is a general movement from Level 1 through to Level 5 as the spiritual cycle of the three stages is unfolded.

The above formulation may appear unnecessarily rigid and formal. In the following chapters the analytical scheme will be used as flexibly as possible as its intention is to release, not to coerce, meaning.

8

The Four Elements

THE GARDEN AND THE DESERT

The natural settings, the gardens and the stony places, in which characters find themselves are created by White, like a Renaissance painter, as a series of symbolic precincts. They are pleasant or malignant *loci*, partly naturalistic, partly emblematical of the emotional and moral content of the scene being acted in them. At the second level of imagery, there is a constant sympathy between characters and their setting, which reflects the flickers, fears, doubts and elations of their secret inner lives. The general tonality of the spot is given harmonic richness by clusters of sub-imagery associated with it. A mood of anguish or of joy is developed and sustained by the connotations of atmospheric conditions, the state of vegetation, and the prevailing aspect of the mineral world. Storms torment the tormented soul and sun releases its tranquillity. Roses evoke the sensuous happiness of childhood, pines, its nostalgia. The stench of crushed herbs or weeds accompanies moments of corrupt emotions or decaying relationships. Blackberries claw and nooses of grass entangle the embattled individual. Dust, sand and rocks replace grass and flowers as fulfilment gives way to deprivation.

Sometimes the change from personal joy to personal sorrow will be reflected in an actual change of scene, as when the garden of Meroë and the 'peace of mind' it represents gives way to the spiky apartness of the *jardin exotique*, or when Rhine Towers is replaced by the desert. But such a physical change is not necessary, since it is the state of mind that releases the pleasant or malignant aspects of the symbolic precinct. Amy Parker experiences the torments of her miscarriage and the fulsome joys of motherhood in a garden that is objectively the same, but of which the emblematic resonances are quite different. The one Sarsaparilla is two quite different countries of the mind for the degenerate Waldo and the saintly Arthur. The devils of Perialos are transformed by Hurtle Duffield into apocalpytic angels, whereas Hero can find only concupiscence and filth.

As the individual passes through a series of apparently only private experiences in these pleasant or malignant spots, the emotional rhythm of a lifetime slowly organizes itself into a larger pattern. The individual, often unconsciously, is participating in a wider human drama (Level 3) which receives symbolic reinforcement from two great archetypes. These archetypes are, on the apocalyptic side, the Garden (or the Garden in its essential forms—the Tree and the Flower), and, on the daemonic side, the Desert, Wasteland or Labyrinth.

In the first phase of its life cycle, the soul inhabits an earthly paradise, wooed into acceptance of the flesh by the sensuous beauty of the natural world. This early Eden is the first essential step in the development of the self, and is marked by complete and joyous acceptance of the existential bond between the 'I' and the phenomenal world, which includes its own body. At this stage, the particular and individual qualities of the garden are more important than its symbolic resonances, although these are always stirring below the surface, reminding the reader of the wider pattern into which the unique situation will eventually blend. Through imagistic suggestion, verbal parallels, echoes or direct comparison, the Eden archetype is evoked at Meroë, Rhine Towers, the Bonners' garden, the Parkers' farm in its early years, Xanadu and, more remotely, the Courtneys' sheep station. 'Kudjeri', for the Hunter children, is a failed or sterile paradise, as is all of Australia. One of White's greater achievements as mythopoeic writer is to take this traditional *locus amoenus* from its place in European art and literature, and graft it onto the Australian soil. But at this stage the echo is muted; the garden is a real garden, the trees and roses are rich in colour, stirring with organic life, redolent and heady.

One of the most important elements of the garden is its sexuality, which throughout White's writing is often associated with vegetable life of one sort or another. The rose at this stage is a fleshly, sensual rose, linked with the sexuality that is part of the seduction of the soul into the body. Rose Portion and Amy Parker are earthly, not heavenly roses. In *The Eye of the Storm*, there is a beautiful prose hymn in celebration of this rose, which also, however, carries a hint of a higher mode of rose life:

As soon as arrived, she began to snatch like a hungry goat. Dew sprinkling around her in showers. Thorns gashing. Her heels tottered obliquely when

not planted in a compost of leaves and sodden earth. Nothing could be done about the worms, lashing themselves into a frenzy of pink exposure: she was too obsessed by her vice of roses. When she stooped to cut into the stems, more than the perfume, the pointed buds themselves could have been shooting up her greedy nostrils, while blown heads, colliding with her flanks, crumbled away, to lie on the neutral earth in clots of cream, splashes of crimson, gentle heart-shaped rose rose . . .
Poured in steadily increasing draughts through the surrounding trees, the light translated the heap of passive rose-flesh back into dew, light, pure colour. It might have saddened her to think her own dichotomy of earthbound flesh and aspiring spirit could never be resolved so logically . . .
(ES p. 209)

The very fact that this paradise is earthly makes its happiness insecure and its joys suspect. It is of this world, and must be imperfect. There is a flaw in the garden, the rose is sick, with a worm at its centre (AS p. 21), Voss is like a serpent sliding into Paradise (V p. 138), and Laura Trevelyan, during a rose-picking ceremony very similar to that of Mary de Santis, is caught on the thorns of an old, staggy rosebush (V p. 170). It is necessary that the flawed and imperfect earthly garden should, of its own nature, perish, leaving the soul, committed almost by guile to the flesh, to pass into the wilderness.

The garden becomes overgrown and tangled, a wasteland, wilderness, labyrinth or desert that threatens the embattled house. The classical pediment of the Browns' house can scarcely hold its own against the jungle by which it is surrounded; Xanadu is slowly crumbling under the assaults of marauding vegetation, while inside, its owner winds through labyrinths of suffering. The drought invades the Parkers' house, while its garden, like the Browns', becomes a wilderness. The desert, into which Mr Bonner had thought Voss was safely exiled, creeps past the fortifications of his mansion.

In the second stage, the central character takes on the archetypal resonances of the Wanderer. In *The Aunt's Story*, the archetypal shadow is Odysseus, while in *The Tree of Man* it is the wanderings of the Jews in the desert. *Voss* captures the historical spirit of the great Australian explorers, and is also in structure like an upside-down *Divine Comedy* where Voss, a perverse Dante, quits the Rose Garden and journeys down through the Earthly Paradise into the burning desert which intensifies its daemonic properties until he reaches what is recognized as the centre of Hell. In *Riders in the Chariot*, Himmelfarb is linked with several Old Testament Jews, with Ahasuerus and, of course, with the wanderings and exiles of Israel. *The Solid Mandala* is underpinned by images of the Wasteland (which, of course, is also

present in *The Living and the Dead*, with its hero Elyot), and the limping
Fisher King can be found both here and in *The Eye of the Storm*. In *The
Vivisector*, images of the labyrinth once more evoke the plight of the
soul lost in the world of experience.

But when the Wanderer is most lost, he finds himself coming home.
Calvary is situated at the centre of Hell. At the moment of death, the
new King is born. God waits at the heart of the labyrinth. The garden,
the trees and the flowers once more appear, but are no longer of the
natural world. The tree becomes the Tree of Life, the flower becomes
the Celestial Rose or the Golden Flower, the garden becomes the
Heavenly Paradise.

This moment is briefly prefigured in *The Living and the Dead* when
the dying Mrs Standish sees a yellow crocus on the window sill (LD
p. 313). The roses that introduce Theodora Goodman to consciousness
in the beginning, and which, in middle life, become only the symbols
of roses on the wallpaper, are transformed, on the last page, into the
black and doubtful rose, living a life of its own on Theodora's hat. In
The Tree of Man, the dying Mrs O'Dowd glimpses a red geranium
blazing on the sill, hinting at resurrection. The Eden that Stan had
found or created in the beginning, and which was taken from him in
middle life, is returned to him in a dying vision. He finds himself at the
centre of a boundless Garden, which is also a terrestrial mirror-image
of the Celestial Rose:

Out there at the back, the grass, you could hardly call it a lawn, had formed a
circle in the shrubs and trees which the old woman had not so much planted as
stuck in during her lifetime. There was little of design in the garden originally,
though one had formed out of the wilderness. It was perfectly obvious that the
man was seated at the heart of it, and from this heart the trees radiated, with
grave movements of life, and beyond them the sweep of a vegetable garden . . .
All was circumference to the centre, and beyond that the worlds of other
circles . . . The last circle but one was the cold and golden bowl of winter,
enclosing all that was visible and material, and at which the man would blink
from time to time, out of his watery eyes, unequal to the effort of realizing that
he was the centre of it. (TM pp. 493–4)

The tree which first appears as Holstius among the pines, and
reappears in *The Tree of Man* as a pledge of renewal and continuity on
the organic plane, figures again in *Voss* and *Riders in the Chariot* with all
the weight of mysticism and myth behind it. In the former case, Voss
sees it in a vision of Jesus reaching down to him from the Southern
Cross (V p. 415), in the latter case, the jacaranda tree on which
Himmelfarb is crucified becomes both the Crucifix and also the
Jewish Tree of Light (RC p. 483).

In *The Solid Mandala*, both Waldo and Arthur are potential bearers of the Golden Flower (the 'dill'), symbol of eternal life, but whereas Arthur realizes the potential, Waldo destroys the Golden Flower. The last image he has as he dies is of Arthur's face falling apart like a 'great marigold' (SM p. 214). Arthur is last seen being taken off to a Home whose garden is so beautiful it has been called 'Peaches-and-Plums'.

The Vivisector ends with the Rose blossoming in Hurtle's dying mind, and the same rose appears, as a symbol for both renewal and transcendence, on the last page of *The Eye of the Storm*. Lotte Lippmann hits on the truth during her song-and-dance routine for Mrs Hunter:

'*Die Rosen können nie vergehen,*
Die Liebe lässt sie neuerstehen . . .' (ES p. 446)

FIRE

As in the philosophy of Heraclitus, the world of Patrick White burns constantly with an inner fire. It is a fire that bursts out from time to time in moments of intense joy or suffering. It is the fire of the inner life, of the emotions, which expresses both the torment and the hidden poetry of the individual. It is also the fire of the soul whose sufferings are purgatorial, whose poetry is finally transformed into revelation.

At the individual level, fire arouses and expresses the capacity of the Unique One to experience an intensity of emotion, both good and bad, unknown to others. Beneath Theodora Goodman's un-prepossessing exterior is a hidden passion, just as the ugly landscape of Meroë or the battered Indian ball contain a secret fire of which she alone is aware. Stan Parker possesses a vein of poetry inside, which he can never express, but which flares up in response to the poetry of the burning Glastonbury, just as Theodora's and Katina's awareness of the danger and ecstasy of music is expressed in the image of the burning piano (AS p. 263).

The fire is intimately related to the core of being in the individual, and to the world of Being behind nature. This Being that runs through and sustains existence can express itself in either ecstasy or agony, or in both simultaneously. Its very capacity to break out of its husk, which exhilarates the soul and gives it a glimpse of a higher reality, is dangerous. It is destructive of individual identity and the life led in houses, in which order and habit prevail. Just as the illusion of personal power, autonomy and control is eroded by the growth of the wilderness or the invasion of the desert, so the ravages of fire expose the illusions of permanence and security behind which characters habitually shelter. At the beginning of *The Tree of Man*, Stan Parker lights a small, reasonable fire. The fire at this stage is an adjunct of the individual will, functional and sustaining, expressing man's need to assert himself against nature. Through the early years, this reasonable fire accompanies the secure lives of the Parkers, contrasting with the uncontrolled blaze of lightning and sunset. As power passes out of his hand, however, the fire of man gets out of control, roaring up in the bush fire, the fire at Glastonbury and finally the War, diminishing man's self-importance while hinting, through its very ferocity, at a magic unknown in mundane existence. Only in old age does the fire die away, to become the nostalgic fire of winter, the burning off of leaves, the raking together of ashes.

As man passes from innocence to experience, he is increasingly exposed to the daemonic attributes of fire, the fire of lust, of evil and of suffering. He passes from the fire of the inner life to the fire of the human situation in its fallen state. In *Riders in the Chariot*, Himmelfarb has a fire-vision which expresses the plight of humanity, racked perpetually by the fires of suffering, in perpetual need of rescue or redemption:

For now that the tops of the trees had caught fire, the bells of the ambulances were again ringing for him, those of the fire-engine clanging, and he shuddered to realize there could never be an end to the rescue of men from the rubble of their own ideas ... So the souls were crying and combing their smoked-out hair. They were already exhausted by the bells, prayers, orders and curses of the many fires at which, in the course of their tormented lives, it had been their misfortune to assist. (RC pp. 344–5)

The fire of experience is the fire of the desert and the fire of the furnace, behind which burns the daemonic archetype of hell-fire. All the local fires of *Riders in the Chariot*, literal and metaphorical, are gathered together and expressed in Alf Dubbo's painting of the Fiery Furnace. In the middle phase of the spiritual cycle, all of White's characters, in one way or another, are cast into this furnace. But the image of the furnace suggests that the fire of suffering is not a permanent condition, but serves a higher end. Suffering, in White, is always teleological. The furnace is the alchemist's crucible, through which the baseness of matter is transmuted into a higher substance—the pure gold, or fire, of the spirit.

The daemonic aspect of fire is related, perhaps, not so much to the permanence of hell-fire as to the transitional fire of purgatory. As was pointed out in Chapter Two, evil ultimately destroys itself, and fire is the symbol of this cleansing process. In *The Aunt's Story*, the fire at the Hôtel du Midi purges Theodora of all her evil or unruly passions and memories, resolving the torments of Part One and preparing her for the final revelations in Part Three, which are also heralded by fire. In *Voss*, the three visionaries must pass through the purgatorial torments of the desert in order that 'the gold may be given up' (V p. 385). In *Riders in the Chariot*, the fiery furnace of earthly suffering is converted into the fiery Chariot of redemption.

The fire of the inner life, which in *The Aunt's Story* is expressed in the image of the sudden fire which blazes up inside the shell of the Indian ball, is also the fire of the soul, the spark hidden at the centre of the core of being. It is the in-dwelling Christ or the *shecchinah* whose sparks have been scattered in the husks of matter and must be released by the Messiah. The fires of the flesh are the purgatorial fires which finally burn away the contamination of external existence, allowing the inner fire to flow back to its source. Daemonic fire serves the end of its polar opposite—Pentecostal Fire, or fire of Divine Revelation. The fire within is released and redeemed by fire.

WATER

The novels from *The Aunt's Story* to *Riders in the Chariot* burn. Their fire is contained within the whole corpus of White's writing like a magnesium flare drifting across a seascape. In the works before and after this great central bonfire it is the spirits of air and water who preside.

The individual experiences the condition of water in his inner life through moments of emotional release. These 'flowing' moments are kindred to, and often expressed simultaneously by, images of fire, music and poetry. Like the moments of fire, they are accompanied by feelings of joy and exhilaration but, because of their intensity and the threat to identity involved, they are also dangerous or destructive moments. It is necessary that the flow should be arrested, that form should re-assert itself. The inner life of the individual alternates between long periods in which form, the body, the led life and normality predominate, and brief interludes in which pure being breaks through. This alternation is suggested by transitions from images that express a condition of stasis, such as wood, stone, sculpture or architecture, to images of flow—water, music and poetry. Only at the very end is it seen that both modes of existence are interchangeable symbols for the spiritual life.

There is a slow shift of meaning in White's use of water symbolism
from the earlier to the later novels. In the first novels, the sea stands
for the numinous world of Being, or its daemonic counterpart—primordial Chaos. By the time we get to *The Vivisector*, however,
water has become the symbol for the material world itself; the ocean
is now the ocean of Time-Space, the world of generation and decay,
concupiscence and greed, and also the unconcscious mind. In *The Eye
of the Storm*, both meanings are present, the sea symbolizing both the
world of *maya* and the endlessness of *Brahman*, of which the individual
life is but a passing wave.

In the novels from *Happy Valley* to *The Tree of Man*, the sea, the mist
or the flood are generalized aspects of that inner capacity to 'flow'
noted above. They are the formless groundswell of Being that contains both the sickness and the ecstasy of which the individual must
force himself to become aware. The sea is a symbol of a higher order
of reality, a unity which expresses itself through cleavage and pain,
but this unity, dissolving, as it does, the individual identity, is feared
by people like Mrs Standish or Amy Parker who seek a narrower, ego-
based definition of reality. Only a few characters can accept the full
implications of their intuitions of this destructive element, characters
like Oliver Halliday, Elyot and Eden Standish, Theodora Goodman
and Stan Parker.

In its destructive mode, its archetype, as found particularly in *The
Tree of Man*, is the water of the Flood, which parallels the fire as
destroyer of houses and the security of lives led in them. For those
who can accept its redemptive power, it is also the water of Baptism;
only by immersion, as Elyot Standish discovers, can rebirth be
achieved.

At the anagogic level of significance, the sea is the sea of eternity
into which the rivers of individual lives must eventually flow. This
level exists only by implication in the early novels. The first three
books end not with death but with existential rebirth, a rebirth which,
in the case of Theodora Goodman, involves turning the back on,
rather than embracing, the eternal circles of spring water. By the time
we come to *The Tree of Man*, the philosophical use of water symbolism
is much less prevalent; it is Mrs O'Dowd, whose spiritual capacity is
rather limited, who is swept away at death by water, whereas Stan
Parker achieves unity with the cosmos through firm geometrical images of form.

As the novels go on, there is an increasing emphasis on water as a
symbol for the condition of man 'drowned' in the material world.
Just as fire, at one level, can be the fire of the flesh, so water can be the

water of the world of experience. The connection between water and the condition of man in the physical world is seen in the Waldo section of *The Solid Mandala*, in which Waldo lives a fearful, under-water life down Terminus Road, threatened by waves of grass and storm cloud. It continues in the 'drowned' existence of the major characters in *The Vivisector*. In this novel, images of water co-operate with images of vegetation, of animals and of filth in various forms to create a dense and unrelieved vision of the plight of man plunged into the world of generation and corruption. This image pattern begins to appear overtly in the conception of 'Lantana Lovers' in which the vegetable world of carnality where lovers are under attack by human and divine perversity is called a 'sea' at several points. It is most fully developed in the Hero Pavloussi section of the novel in which Hurtle has reached the nadir of his descent into matter, and is beginning to turn upward again towards the light. The drowning of the Pavloussis' cats by the disillusioned Cosma impels Hurtle to paint 'Infinity of Cats' which continues the line of thought begun in 'Lantana Lovers'. It shows the parallel between the plight of these unlovely animals being drowned in the name of love by a wilful human being, and the plight of himself and Hero in particular, and humanity in general, being cast into the ocean of existence by an apparently equally arbitrary Deity. (This image appears again in *The Eye of the Storm*, where two little girls throw dolls into a river; throughout the book characters are referred to as 'dolls', thus suggesting the parallel between infantile and divine sport.)

At the end of the Hero chapter, however, Hurtle glimpses the sea in a different mode. During their visit to Perialos, Hero can see only filth and degradation, but the artist at her side becomes aware that the material world and its emblem the ocean have a beauty which, if it could only be seen, confirms the existence of the God that Hero is seeking in vain elsewhere. Beauty in the fallen world—a beauty which often only the artist can see, being immune from the usual categories of 'the pretty' and 'the ugly'—is the signature of God and the pledge of renewal:

He was conscious of God as a formal necessity on which depended every figure in the afternoon's iconography . . . The ouzo in him, which should have helped dissolve, made him cling, on the contrary, to outward and visible signs . . . (Viv p. 404)

It was Hero who might have drunk the ouzo. She was drunk, but with her disillusion and helplessness . . . He would have liked to point out the scaly sea, like a huge, live fish, rejoicing in its evening play . . . (Viv p. 406)

All this time a little golden hen had been stalking and clucking . . . The warm scallops of her golden feathers were of that same inspiration as the scales of the great silver-blue sea creature they—or he, at least—had watched from John of the Apocalypse, ritually coiling and uncoiling before dissolving in the last light.

'See—Hero?' he began to croak, while pointing with his ineffectual finger. 'This hen!' he croaked.

Hero half-directed her attention at the hen; but what he could visualize and apprehend, he could really only convey in paint, and then not for Hero. The distressing part was: they were barking up the same tree. (Viv pp. 408–9)

The sea with its cargo of monstrous spawn continues to flood through the veins of *The Eye of the Storm*. It is now a symbol for the fallen world and also for the chthonic depths of the unconscious mind. Elizabeth Hunter has always been at home in, and mistress of, the destructive element. She identifies herself with the 'skiapod', a mythical creature with the body of a fish and the rather sly face of a woman, and both her sexuality and her greed are expressed through marine images. (The same symbolism appears, in all its scaly beauty and horror, during the scene in San Fabrizio in 'Sicilian Vespers' quoted in part in an earlier chapter.) It is fitting that the dying skiapod should experience a sea change in her drowned depths, in which all the experiences of her carnivorous life are transformed into an underwater nightmare. Her purgatory, unlike that of the Riders, is not composed of fire but of water, and the daemons of her resurrection are the crab, the shark and the octopus. At the moment of death, she experiences both the daemonic and the baptismal aspects of water as, threatened by Chaos, she hurries to immerse herself in the ocean of pure Being:

Now the real business in hand was not to withdraw her will, as she had once foreseen, but to will enough strength into her body to put her feet on the ground and walk steadily towards the water. There was the question of how much time she would have before the eye must concentrate on other, greater contingencies, leaving her to chaos. That this was threatening, she could tell from the way the muslin was lifted at the edges, till what had been a benison of sea, sky, and land, was becoming torn by animal passions, those of a deformed octopod with blue-suckered tentacles and a glare of lightning or poached eggs.

To move the feet by some miraculous dispensation to feel sand benign and soft between the toes the importance of the decision makes the going heavy at first the same wind stirring the balconies of cloud as blows between the ribs it would explain the howling of what must be the soul not for fear that it will blow away in any case it will but in anticipation of its first experience of precious water as it filters in through the cracks the cavities of the body blue pyramidal waves

with swans waiting by appointment . . . to end in legend is what frightens most
people more than cold water climbing mercifully towards the overrated but
necessary heart . . .
. . . let us rather—enfold.
Till I am no longer filling the void with mock substance: myself is this
endlessness. (ES pp. 550–1)

AIR

Like earth, fire and water, the air has a double nature, simultaneously
destructive and redemptive. Death by air joins death by fire and death
by water as an aspect of the world of experience, but this death at the
level of individual existence releases the breath within to a higher
mode of being in the 'immense fields of silence' (V p. 405). At the
archetypal level, air is the Whirlwind of God which both Moses and
Ezekiel saw. But it is also the small voice of calm at the centre of
the whirlwind. Just as hell-fire can be transformed into Pentecostal
Fire, so too the destructiveness of the storm can be transformed into
the gentleness of the Holy Ghost, the Spirit that moves as it lists.

The wind, the storm and the sky corrode the identity and self-
importance of the individual. In *The Tree of Man*, storms act in conjunction with flood and fire to make man aware of the narrow boundaries of his potency. The sky is too vast, the lightning too fierce, the
wind too powerful for him. The first storm begins by exhilarating
Stan Parker, but ends by humbling him as his initial delight in and
empathy with its strength turns into a sense of helplessness. The
traumatic impact of the storm upon the pretensions of the individual
is shown even more vividly, of course, in *The Eye of the Storm*, where the
whirlwind Jehovah destroys the house with a flick of His finger and
reduces the arrogant Elizabeth Hunter to a shred of skin and bone
cowering on a shelf.

Just as man dwindles to an insignificant dot in the face of the
vastness of the sky or the fury of the storm, so his hopes for personal
happiness are blown away by the wind's erosion:

Standing upon the steps of the church, in the high wind, Laura Trevelyan
watched her cousin, in whose oblivious arms lay the sheaf of black sticks, of
which the flowerets threatened to blow away, bearing with them tenderly,
whitely, imperceptibly, the myth of all happiness. (V p. 352)

The daemonic actions of air are not just external threats, however.
The storm also blows through the temperament and spins characters

into the maddened vortex of social behaviour. It is the 'gale of life' that batters the tree of man and causes such distress to thin souls like Thelma Forsdyke. *The Eye of the Storm* is structured like a cyclone, of which the driving force is the turbulent emotion and unquiet passion that spins all the characters around the centre, a centre which itself revolves fiercely under the lashes of guilt. The carnage caused by these inner storms is, in human terms, even greater than that caused by the actual cyclone that hits Brumby Island.

But the very existence of the Whirlwind brings with it the suggestion of the still, small voice at the centre—the Eye which is also the 'I'. The erosion of the wind and the vastness of the sky hint at the release of spiritual power and the potential infinity of the soul. These are there for those who, like Laura Trevelyan or Mrs Hunter, can accept the destruction of individuality or have the strength to endure until the Eye is reached. At the beginning of Laura's relationship with Voss, before she has fully descended into flesh:

She would have liked to sit upon a rock and listen to words, not of any man, but detached, mysterious, poetic words that she alone would interpret through some sense inherited from sleep. Herself disembodied. Air joining air experiences a voluptuousness no less intense because imperceptible. (V p. 68)

At this early stage, such a desire is a symptom of Laura's immature spiritual condition, but as her experience deepens, and she learns first the joy of the flesh through the birth of Mercy, and then its suffering, from the death of Rose, the wisdom of air becomes a reality to her:

... what of her own expectant soul, or tender roseflesh of the child? Each grain of merciless sand suggested to the girl that her days of joy had been, in a sense, illusory ... There was such a swirling and whirling that the earth itself pulled loose, all was moving, and the mourners lowered their heads, and braced their feeble legs to prevent themselves from being sent spinning.

... After the first shock of discovery, it had been exhilarating to know that terrestrial safety is not assured, and that solid earth does eventually swirl beneath the feet. Then, when the wind had cut the last shred of flesh from the girl's bones, and was whistling in the little cage that remained, she began even to experience a shrill happiness, to sing the wounds her flesh would never suffer. Yet, such was their weakness, her bones continued to crave earthly love, to hold his skull against the hollow where her heart had been. It appeared that pure happiness must await the final crumbling, when love would enter into love, becoming an endlessness, blowing at last, indivisible, indistinguishable, over the brown earth. (V p. 251)

The power of the spirit to transcend terrestrial limitations is revealed by the nature of the relationship between Laura and Voss. After Dugald tears up Voss's last letter and throws it to the wind, this relationship is truly one of air joining air, or spirit joining spirit. After the flesh has gone, communion still remains.

As the wind releases and expresses the spiritual power of the inner life, so the sky symbolizes the vast world of Being to which the breath finally returns. In *Voss*, this is expressed in terms of aboriginal eschatology, and the hallucinated explorers have visions of the soul escaping into the circles of the sky like a bird. *The Vivisector* ends with Hurtle painting God as an infinite expanse of blue—the colour that also appears in both malignant and sacramental forms in *Riders in the Chariot*, and gives Himmelfarb his name. The curtains in Mrs Hunter's room blow uncontrollably as the soul of the dead woman escapes into the night.

The sky is, perhaps, the most adequate of all symbols of the Hidden God; air is, of all aspects of the phenomenal world, the most devoid of content, providing the least obstruction to the mystery of Being. Other symbols with more overt substance of their own conceal as much as they reveal in their effort to express the true nature of Divinity. Air is the least anthropomorphic expression of the God from Whom all substance emanates, but Who is Himself without substance.

9

The Lamb, the Temple
and the Sun

ANIMALS

There is a key symbolic configuration of ant, man and sun in *The Tree of Man* (TM pp. 46, 290, 412, 497) which graphically portrays the condition of humanity in this and, indeed, all White's novels. This conjunction shows the unity of Being that runs through all things, the cosmic bonfire that burns alike in the source of fire and the smallest created particle, and which comes to consciousness in man. It also exposes dramatically the predicament of man, suspended half-way between ant and sun, or matter and spirit. As man looks down on the struggling ants, he becomes aware of his own situation under the eyes of God. Looking up at the sun, he speculates on the nature of this God Who controls man's life as man controls that of the animal world. Able to comprehend the nature of Divinity only by analogy with his own wilful or arbitrary treatment of animals, he is shaken, like Stan Parker, or outraged, like Hurtle Duffield, by the ruthlessness of Divine logic. 'As flies to wanton boys are we to the gods; they kill us for their sport' can be heard by implication in all the bewildered musings on the nature of God that are to be found in White's novels.

Animal life proliferates below the human level in White's pages—a riot of insects, cats, dogs, horses, sheep, cows, goats and birds. By contrast and correspondence, it reveals the human condition in its fallen state, the state of separation from the light. In this section, four related aspects of the animal condition will be selected to reflect the plight of humanity, and a resolution of man's predicament that also emerges from the animal images will be suggested. The first significant attribute of the animal world is its carnal, beastly or chthonic nature, the second is its capacity to give or arouse love or affection, the third is its defencelessness in the hands of cruel and arbitrary mankind and the fourth is its innocence.

Animals are symbols of the lower half of man's incarnate nature—the blood, the passions, the instincts and the sexuality. They can also express the squalor, filth and unthinking viciousness of man when he is farthest away from God. In *The Tree of Man*, Amy's outburst of sexuality is accompanied by the appearance of a yellow dog and the lascivious attentions of a tomcat. In *The Solid Mandala*, the rambunctious and obscene activities of Scruffy and Runt embody the instinctual side of life from which Waldo shrinks in fascinated loathing. In *Voss*, horses often act as symbols for the lower half of man's nature, as in this passage, in which Laura controls her horse as her will controls her emotions:

'And here is Mr Voss himself,' . . .
Laura did turn then, too suddenly, for it alarmed her horse into springing sideways. But she was moulded to it by her will . . .

'Laura, can you control her?' called the frightened Belle.
'Yes,' breathed Laura Trevelyan, on her calmer, but still trembling, mare.

And she continued to sit sculpturally upon her mastered horse, of which the complicated veins were throbbing with blood and frustration. (V pp. 116–17)

In *The Vivisector*, cats reveal the squalor and degradation that are inherent in the depths of man's nature. They support the other images of disgust with carnality. Two possible attitudes of God towards man are suggested by the drowning of cats by Cosma Pavloussi and the nurture of cats by the equally disillusioned but persevering Rhoda Courtney. The action of *The Solid Mandala* closes with the symbolic devouring of Waldo by the despised dogs, who now appear as avenging gods of the underworld.

As was pointed out in Chapter Three, carnality and love are closely allied, since compassion is a virtue of some sensual origin. Animals have a capacity for affection and devotion which mirrors the same quality in the lower aspect of the human personality, and which the Nous principle must learn to accept before true love of God can be discovered. Voss is aware of this quality in his dogs which are devoted to him and for which, in spite of himself, he feels affection. For this very reason the obsessed German shoots his favourite dog Gyp (V pp. 254–5). The murder of the dog is, in psychological fact, an attempt to repress the Laura aspect of his own nature—his need to give and receive love.

The shooting of Gyp highlights a third aspect of the animal condition—its vulnerability to the evil or perverse impulses of man. Animals are always seen as victims in White's novels, and there is a long catalogue of maimed or murdered beasts. We find the staked dog in *The Living and the Dead*, the hawk Theodora Goodman shoots, the puppies and birds that Ray Parker kills, the beasts Voss takes on his expedition, the rooster and snake that Hadkin and Mrs Jolley kill in *Riders in the Chariot*, the numerous victims of man's cruelty, thoughtlessness or misplaced idealism in *The Vivisector*, the staked gull and murdered lovebird in *The Eye of the Storm* and the crippled cockatoo that is beaten to death at the end of 'The Cockatoos'. But—as *The Vivisector* sets out to demonstrate—the knife that slaughters the animal is never far distant from the human throat as well. The butchered animal is an emblem for the universal law of suffering that afflicts man too. In spite of his arrogance, man is the universal victim.

The fourth attribute of the animal world, in which it differs from that of man, is its essential innocence. Some animals, like the cows which are at the symbolic heart of the innocent pastoral life of the Parkers, are singled out for this very quality, but all, even the most rampantly sexual or disgusting, live purely instinctual lives and are, at the very worst, morally neutral. They live and die obeying the law of necessity, in harmony with their nature and Nature in general, and they know nothing of evil, even when their behaviour might, if translated onto the human plane, appear evil. Evil comes about only when one is capable of rising above and perverting the laws of necessity—a power which man alone possesses, through his kinship with God. Man is not instinctual and innocent; this is his curse and (in its most spiritual sense) his saving grace. Those who live only in the body can only die. The significance of this observation is made clear in the case of Mary Hare. Her retreat from the human to the animal world is a retreat from cruelty and perversity to innocence, but her spiritual destiny cannot be fulfilled until she has been brought back into the human world and has come to terms with the evil that resides there and is also lodged in her own heart. Only a human being could practise the forms of cruelty that Mary finds herself practising; only a human being would pass through fire for a friend.

This brings us to the final point: the redeemability of man's bestial condition. As man is saved by fire from fire, and from air by air, so his animality is redeemed by a higher function of its own nature. The awareness of evil and suffering, which is uniquely granted to man, allows him to take upon himself the full spiritual consequences of his animal nature: its love, its suffering and its execution. The apocalyptic archetype of the animal is the beast of sacrifice—the Lamb, the Hare or the Scapegoat. Many of White's victims are smitten down without ever becoming aware of what has struck them, like the 'pole-axed' Harry Courtney. Others desperately try to evade their role as a sacrifice. The best example of this is Judd, whose determination not to be offered up is humanly admirable but spiritually limiting:

> The man-animal joined them and sat for a while upon the scorching bank. It was possibly this communion with the beasts that did finally rouse his bemused human intellect, for in their company he sensed the threat of the knife, never far distant from the animal throat.
> 'I will not! I will not!' he cried at last, shaking his emaciated body.
> Since his own fat paddocks, not the deserts of mysticism, nor the transfiguration of Christ, are the fate of common man, he was yearning for the big breasts of his wife. (V pp. 367–8)

But it is 'the transfiguration of Christ' that redeems man from his purely fleshly condition, and this can be achieved, not by avoiding the sacrificial knife, but by the act of self-sacrifice. The law of suffering is overcome by the power of love in those who, like Laura, Himmelfarb, Mary Hare or Arthur Brown, willingly take the full charge of suffering to themselves. Only by this act of acceptance, by the heroic act of self-renunciation, does the voluntary Lamb rise above His earthly state. In the light shed by this last act of sacrifice, it is revealed that the knife which slit the animal throat released the human soul.

It is now that the second aspect of the double-natured bird image comes into its own. While participating in and sharing all the other qualities of the animal kingdom, the bird is also the symbol for the purely spiritual side of man's nature. It is the part of man which descends, like Leda's swan or Mary's Dove, and takes up its abode in the flesh. It is the side which, after the cage of bones is broken, 'enfolds' the soul, like Elizabeth Hunter's black swans, or soars into the circles of the sky, like the bird-souls of *Voss*. Its flight links the spirit with the Holy Spirit. It is thus that we find it in the lyrical conclusion of *The Eye of the Storm*, where all the dark experiences of the book are dissolved into a vision of light and wings:

> In the garden the first birds were still only audible shadows, herself an ambulant tree.
> The hem of her nightdress soon became saturated, heavy as her own flesh, as she filled the birds' dishes. Reaching up, her arms were rounded by increasing light.
>
> Light was strewing the park as she performed her rites. Birds followed her, battering the air, settling on the grass whenever her hand, trembling in the last instant, spilt an excess of seed.

She poured the remainder of the seed into the dish on the upper terrace. The birds already clutching the terracotta rim, scattered as she blundered amongst them, then wheeled back, clashing, curving, descending and ascending, shaking the tassels of light or seed suspended from the dish. She could feel claws snatching for a hold in her hair.

She ducked, to escape from this prism of dew and light, this tumult of wings and her own unmanageable joy. Once she raised an arm to brush aside a blue wedge of pigeon's feathers. The light she could not ward off: it was by now too solid, too possessive; herself possessed. (ES p. 608)

HOUSES

White's characters wear their houses as intimately as they wear their bodies. Houses, from the hugger-mugger to the impeccable, from the honestly functional to the decadently baroque, are almost inextricably woven into the lives of their owners. White takes endless delight in the colours and textures, the sounds and smells, the decor and mood of all types and conditions of houses; his collector's enthusiasm and architectural verve make his house-building one of the most memorable aspects of his descriptive power. In almost every page of the writing, the reader is aware of the almost organic link between the house and the emotional life of its occupant. Houses live the lives of their owners, reflecting their pretensions or their honesty, their squalor or their opulence, their conformity or their fantasy. Their topography reveals the topography of the soul. Thus Tallboys, in *The Solid Mandala*, reflects the social mask of the individual in its Palladian facade, the ego in its Tudor living quarters and the unconscious in its (Gothic Folly'. The contrasting and counterpointing of different houses highlights the qualities and shortcomings of different life styles and spiritual conditions. Thus *Voss* progresses from the Bonners' mansion to the Sandersons' simple house, to the squalor of Jildra and, after reaching the nadir in a rudimentary twig hut, returns to the Bonners' which is now enriched by the whole experience of the novel. White's sensitivity to the auras and emanations of houses makes them an almost infinitely flexible language for the expression of many areas of existence that reason cannot reach.

The function of the house is to give substance and security to the life of its owner as the body does for the soul. But the act of embodiment is also an act of limitation. Behind the image of the house lies the daemonic archetype of the Prison-Fortress. The 'led life' is given structure by the house, but this house is constantly under siege by the various faces of Chaos discussed in the last chapter. Man's four-square, ego-based life is constantly threatened by fire, flood, storm and the wasteland—symbols for the suffering and ecstasy inherent in the world of Being. Mr Bonner's house, which was intended to be a monument to his own magnificence, becomes an embattled citadel against the suffering which money cannot buy off. The Brown's house is swamped by a sea of vegetation. Norbert Hare's Coleridgean folly is threatened by the cynicism of native shrub. Worse even than these assaults is the fact that by fortifying himself, man has also imprisoned himself. The house that man builds to protect himself against formlessness cuts him off from the spiritual release that this formlessness represents. Man is a prisoner in his house as he is a prisoner in his body. Elyot Standish, for example, who retreats into his room to escape from the complexities and dangers of the emotional life, finds himself increasingly trapped in his cell and yearns for release into the life of the streets which is now not seen as a menace but as a source of renewal.

It is possible, however, that the Prison-Fortress can be transformed into its apocalyptic opposite. As the house is stripped of its pretensions and hypocrisies, as its defences are pierced and the icons to the ego and to social class are laid waste, it may be changed into the Temple. The soul comes into its own as the body begins to decay or to decline from its habitual functions. This transformation is brought about by the acts of worship which are performed in the Temple. The nature of these acts of worship, or of 'testifying', will be dictated by the core of being, which may express itself in prayer, in art, in love, in sacrifice or even (as with Theodora) simply in being itself. Such worship will come most easily when the house is at its most rudimentary (like the derelict shack at the end of *The Aunt's Story*) or dilapidated (like Xanadu or the Browns' house). Stan Parker discovers this truth during the War years:

I sat awhile in a church in one of the villages here last week. It was what remained of a church. It was all sky. There were the frames of the windows, but the glass had fallen . . . There was a wind blowing, and rain, and dogs coming in . . . There was an old woman in that church, skin and bone, praying as if she had just begun to pray. (TM p. 205)

The same point is made even more explicitly in the quotation from Dostoevsky with which White opens *The Solid Mandala*:

It was an old and rather poor church, many of the ikons were without setting, but such churches are the best for praying in.

Where the trappings of external existence are most eroded, essence can assert itself. At the time of Himmelfarb's crucifixion, Norbert Hare's 'pleasure dome' is converted into the temple at Jerusalem. George Brown's 'classical pediment' only succeeds in drawing a parallel between his rational house and a temple.

The once intimate link between the house and its occupant falls apart as time passes. The soul, it emerges at the end, has only been 'wearing' the body; it is not completely identified with it. The same is true of the house and its owner. With the exception of Stan Parker, White's major characters have not created their own houses. They live in the houses of others, which they have 'borrowed', bought, inherited or co-opted by right of imagination. They all make a deeper emotional or spiritual commitment to their adopted houses than the 'true' or original owner, but in no case can it be said of the house that it is truly theirs. And in the end the house must split open like a shell to release its occupant into the realm of Being which has already been glimpsed through the cracks in the walls. At the climactic moment in each novel the house is quitted. Elyot Standish and the Young Man leave their Ebury Street womb, Theodora retreats even from her lonely shack, which has now become a trap, and Stan Parker has his last vision in the boundless garden between the ants and the sun. Voss is executed in the most rudimentary symbol of a house, but 'his dreams fled into the air, his blood ran out upon the dry earth' (V p. 419). Mary Hare leaves Xanadu and Himmelfarb's house is burned to the ground. Waldo, the lower soul, dies in the house, but Arthur, the higher soul, does not die the death of the body but flies from the house. Hurtle Duffield brings the sky into his room in his last painting, while Elizabeth Hunter, who has already withdrawn from almost all of her house and her body, is swirled into the sky in a gust of air. The earthly temple must finally be destroyed, to be replaced by the architecture of Eternity.

SUN AND MOON

The sun and moon preside respectively over the higher and the lower aspects of man and the cosmos. The sun is Nous, the source and the goal of spirit. It is the one, the reason, the masculine principle and, by grace of the English language, the Son. The moon governs the world of matter, of sexuality and generation, the unconscious mind and dreams. Both sun and moon are functions of the soul and aspects of God. Both have their destructive phases, but both can also be agents of redemption. The spirit originates in the sun and passes to the womb of earth through the vessel of the fertile moon. The spirit is then raised up from the earth by the regenerative power of light and finally returns to its source in the third planet or Celestial Sun.

The moon participates in the individual experience as it encounters carnality in its many forms. It shines as Theodora Goodman waits for Frank Parrott under the apricot tree and for Stan and Amy as they make love on their wedding night. The same moon, in its daemonic aspect, haunts Amy during her miscarriage, and its sticky moonlight merges with Waldo Brown's night thoughts or Ruth Godbold's visit to the brothel. In *The Vivisector*, it is the dominating symbol of 'Lantana Lovers', shitting on the lovers in an obscene parody of parturition. The moon bears the implications of all the filth, as well as the fertility, of the carnal world.

The moon governs the unconscious, sleep and dreams. In *Voss*, the moons over Jildra (V p. 189) embody the content of men's dreams, in particular Voss's sleep-conceived scheme to hide the compass in Judd's saddle-bag. In *The Solid Mandala*, it appears in many places as a symbol of the lower world and the unconscious: it is the moons of ice that Arthur dreams in the beginning, the moon on the pierrot bottle, the moon of Tennyson's poem and the 'Moonlight Sonata'. Arthur can accept all these phases of the moon, but Waldo, with his fear of the chthonic, rejects or ignores. He can no more bring the unconscious to the light than he can sustain the full glare of the sun; Waldo's section is full of dim half-light.

The orange disc of the sun, as the epigraph to *The Solid Mandala* suggests, is man's source and his destination: '... *yet still I long for my twin in the sun*'. In *The Tree of Man*, where God is experienced in His aspect of cosmic unity, the sun is a distant symbol of the Hidden God, suggesting by conjunction with other images the fire that burns in the One and the Many. In *Voss* and *Riders in the Chariot*, both the god within and the transcendental God are experienced more personally; just as Christ reveals Himself more overtly in these novels, so the sun swings closer to man, threatening him with destruction and salvation. The 'tigerish sun' of *Voss* (V p. 171) and the Sun-Chariot, whose sunset terror sends Mary Hare into fits, give man a brief glimpse of the absolute power of God.

The terror of the sun and the squalor of the moon are limited to the world of experience, the second stage of the spiritual cycle. Seen correctly, both sun and moon are agents of redemption. The One descends to the world of generation, from which it is redeemed by the light of the third planet, which in the individual is the soul and in the cosmos is the Hidden God. Arthur Brown, the true alchemist, manages to reconcile sun and moon—the conscious and unconscious minds—and by his acceptance of both these spheres he produces the final, the third sphere of the Self, symbolized by the last mandala.

The power of light to regenerate matter is demonstrated throughout *The Vivisector*, where the artist's eye perceives the constant transformation of the mundane into the beautiful by the action of sunlight. This transformation of the drab or ugly into aesthetic beauty is a terrestrial analogy for the transfiguration of the soul. We find it expressed in several places in the novel through Hurtle's wonder at the miracle of the mote:

An almost summer sunlight slatted the floor of the room over Chubb's Lane . . . For him, the light created something festive in his familiar but probably frowsy surroundings. To remember that a flight of motes was of the same substance as passive grey domestic dust had always delighted him. (Viv p. 362)

The most complete expression of the part that moon and sun play in the spiritual cycle is found in a passage in *Voss*, a passage which looks forward prophetically to the appearance of the Comet, whose supernal light rewards the three visionaries for their perseverance:

Riding down the other side, the young man conceived a poem, in which the silky seed that fell in milky rain from the Moon was raised up by the Sun's laying his hands upon it. His flat hands, with their conspicuously swollen knuckles, were creative, it was proved, if one dared accept their blessing. One did dare, and at once it was seen that the world of fire and the world of ice were the same world of light; whereupon, for the first time in history, the third, and dark planet was illuminated. (V p. 268)

10

The Chariot and the Mandala

The images that have been discussed have an obvious on-going existence in the material world from which they are appropriated at certain points to reflect an inner or a higher reality. But there is a line of imagery in White's novels, culminating in the Chariot and the mandalas, of which the naturalistic function is minimal. These images are plucked near their roots in the 'real' world and have an almost purely talismanic or hieratic role. It must be stressed that these images are not imposed on the novels by the author. There is a difference only of degree between these and other images; the psychological or spiritual processes through which they become windows or mirrors of the truth are the same in all cases. The Chariot and the mandalas are simply the most intense manifestation of the symbolizing powers that White's major characters have, just as the crucifixion in *Riders in the Chariot* is the most extreme expression of the myth-making capacity which characters in all the novels possess. Both symbols begin their careers from natural origins. The Chariot is discovered in a chance remark, a painting, a hymn and an occult text, the mandala in children's marbles. In the first stage of the cycle, they are 'real' in the same way as the garden is real in the beginning. These hints or encounters give the characters a premonition of something larger than their individual experience, a premonition that is confirmed as their experience deepens. Once glimpsed, the image is irrevocably lodged in the mind, and as spiritual awareness extends it is embodied in this central symbol which grows as the inner life grows and becomes increasingly autonomous. In the beginning it had been contained by the individual but during the second phase it comes to dominate or possess the characters, as in Mary Hare's visions or Arthur Brown's dance. By the end its power has become so great that it absorbs the individuality of the protagonists into itself carrying them onto a higher plane of reality.

Both the mandala and the Chariot have an ancestry in White's earlier writing, which will emerge as this discussion develops. They grow out of a line of imagery which, if more naturalistic, serves the same emotional and spiritual function. These images are clear-cut, sharp-edged objects, that stand out in relief from their surroundings. They are typified by their brightness, their colour and their beauty, often being linked with precious stones or metals and frequently round in shape. They give the individual a glimpse of something strange and precious which raises the senses to a higher level and arouses some hitherto dormant faculty that is untouched by its generally drab surroundings. They are the focus of the inner life, an external expression of the sense of mystery and poetry which lies nearest the soul.

This radiance exists in the pebbles that Elyot Standish discovers as a boy at Ard's Bay, which continue to glitter in his memory even during the epoch of living death. In *The Aunt's Story*, we find the Indian ball in Part One and the nautilus shell in Part Two. Amy Parker's silver nutmeg grater, the pebble that Bub Quigley holds in his hand during the flood and the fragment of stained glass that the lost boy from the same flood holds up to the firelight, all have the qualities of magical talismans. In *Voss*, the compass acts in a similar way for Judd, although here the functional aspect of the magical object perfectly suggests the limitations of Judd's sensibility. It is the Comet that the three dying visionaries glimpse at the end of this novel that is the most immediate and most striking predecessor of the Chariot.

The radiance that breaks through the mundane crust with the appearance of these objects is, like the radiance of the 'timeless moments' discussed earlier, a fragile and fleeting beauty, which flashes out for a moment before the object is dulled, lost or broken. The vein of poetry that runs through the universe and wells up in the soul of man is glimpsed only briefly before the husk hardens again. Elyot's pebbles lose their sheen when they are brought home, the nautilus shell is smashed when claims of ownership are made on it, Amy's nutmeg grater is lost or stolen, Mary Hare's favourite chandelier is shot to pieces by her father. By their very nature such blazing moments cannot be coerced or possessed; they can only be experienced and remembered.

The response to these talismans suggests the intensely personal and private nature of the inner vision possessed by the 'elect'. At the same time, particularly in the cases of the Chariot and the mandalas, they do not only express the estrangement of the unique individual from the society around him; they are also symbols of the union and com-munion that exist among people of a similar inner grace. In all of his novels after *The Tree of Man*, White is more interested in the possibility of relationship than in the condition of isolation. The emphasis is no longer on 'loneliness' but on 'dialogue'; it is not the barriers between people that interest him, but the moments when these barriers are broken down. The Chariot and the mandalas are vehicles of and symbols for true dialogue between souls. The predominant mood in White is not estrangement but fellowship as seen in the fellowships of the Chariot and the Mandala. This community of souls is given formal expression by Alf Dubbo in his final painting of the 'Chariot-sociable', showing the four Living Creatures sitting face-to-face, and in Arthur's mandala dance that binds together the lives of the four main characters, uniting them in the central image of Christ. The main symbols work centripetally, drawing the lives of the four chief characters together, giving them a corporate identity that allows them to transcend the boundaries of self.

Thus the Chariot and the mandalas give external form to the spiritual life of the individuals who perceive their significance. At the same time they give a corporeal and visible form to the mystery of the God Above; they point simultaneously to the immanent and the transcendent Deity, and in doing so they symbolize the ultimate unity of the two.

The Chariot has two aspects, which reflect the two faces of the Hidden God as He is experienced in all the novels. First, it is a manifestation or revelation of God in his attributes of Majesty and Terror. In the first stage of his spiritual cycle, man is not deeply concerned with either the existence or the nature of the Above. He is himself a pseudo-god and is content with his assumed power to control or create his own destiny. As pseudo-Paradise is laid waste, however, man is forced to give more thought—usually resentful—to the author of Fatality. Writhing under the law of suffering, man discovers that the ultimate affliction of man is the existence of God. Struggling through the wasteland, man is unaware what God's destiny for him is, and so he imagines an evil Deity, a Jehovah who inflicts suffering on man and through man for no apparent reason. Evil, it appears, is directed by God, and so man creates an anthropomorphic God who directs this evil. The God that man images is a lower Deity. He is like the Gnostic demiurge or the cruel Urizen of Blake's system. He is the fiery Jehovah with whom Stan Parker wrestles for much of his life. Stan blames God rather than Amy for the latter's adultery; his impulse, when he discovers it, is not to reject or murder his wife, but to reject God. God's hand in human evil is suggested early to Stan by the warning of an old pedlar:

'. . . the Almighty 'asn't yet shown 'Is 'and. You 'ave not been 'it over the
'ead, kicked downstairs, spat at in the eye. See?' (TM p. 36)

In *The Vivisector*, Hurtle conceives a cruel and vindictive God who is
a projection of all the resentment and bitterness of a man stung by
suffering and by guilt of the suffering he has caused others. From
Nance's death through most of his life, Hurtle has an image of God
that expresses all the outrage of mankind writhing under the destiny
of an unknown despot. He expresses this view of God in two paintings. In one, he shows lovers making love among lantana while the
moon shits on them. In the other he shows God as Cosma Pavloussis
drowning cats. He explains 'Lantana Lovers' to Hero in the following
terms:

'I met the bloke one evening on this bench. He had something rotten about
him, but only slightly, humanly rotten in the light of the Divine Destroyer. I
mean the grocer's attempts at evil are childlike beside the waves of enlightened
evil proliferating from above . . .' (Viv p. 350)

This same God appears in *The Eye of the Storm*, wrapped in the power
and destruction of the whirlwind.

The Chariot of much of *Riders in the Chariot* is a manifestation of this
lower or limited aspect of God. He reveals Himself in air raids, in fits
and frenzies, in the Fiery Furnace or in the slow grinding wheel of a
cart that splits Rob Godbold's head like a melon. But this Urizen-
god, God of the tiger, is not all of the Deity. It is only the face of God
that man sees in the desert. The Chariot, as Himmelfarb knows all
along, is not only the Throne of the King, but also the symbol of the
King's Grace. It is the Chariot of redemption as well as the Chariot of
destruction.

As man passes out of the desert, the despotic overlord gives way to a
purer, less anthropomorphic God, as found in Stan Parker's image of
cosmic unity, in the beauty of the Comet, in Hurtle's last painting of
Indigod and in Elizabeth Hunter's experience of the Eye. The apparently evil element in God is only a partial aspect of His nature, and
serves a higher end. The 'stroke' of God is the medical stroke that kills
Hurtle (God the Vivisector), the brush stroke as God paints through
Hurtle (God the Artist)—but it is also a caress. Hurtle cannot finish
his inscription, but the last page of *The Vivisector* strongly suggests
'God the Redeemer.' Evil is an aspect of God's mercy. While man is in
the middle of the operation with no anaesthetic, he can only resent
and revile whoever is wielding the scalpel. But in the end he is 'cured';

without the nails the Crucifixion could not have happened. Simone Weil gives a prose exposition of this idea, T. S. Eliot a poetic one:

God's mercy is manifest in affliction as in joy, by the same right; more perhaps, because under this form it has no human analogy. Man's mercy is only shown in giving joy, or maybe in inflicting pain with a view to outward results, bodily healing or education. But it is not the outward results of affliction which bear witness to divine mercy. The outward results of true affliction are nearly always bad. We lie when we try to disguise this. It is in affliction itself that the splendour of God's mercy shines; from its very depths, in the heart of its inconsolable bitterness. If still persevering in our love, we fall to the point where the soul cannot keep back the cry 'My God, why hast thou forsaken me?' if we remain at this point without ceasing to love, we end by touching something which is not affliction, which is not joy, something which is the central essence, necessary and pure; something not of the senses, common to joy and sorrow; something which is the very love of God.[17]

> *The wounded surgeon plies the steel*
> *That questions the distempered part;*
> *Beneath the bleeding hands we feel*
> *The sharp compassion of the healer's art*
> *Resolving the enigma of the fever chart.*[18]

In the progress of the Chariot we can see the original rousing of man's spiritual life by contact with images which are experienced naturalistically, through a condition of subjugation to a lower aspect of that image in the world of experience, to final redemption of this bondage by the same symbol as it reflects a higher aspect of God—God as experienced as Grace rather than terror.

The mandala, symbol of the totality of the self and the unity of the individual with the cosmos, crystallizes out of many clues, hints and premonitions in the other novels. It has an obvious ancestry in the bright talismanic objects already mentioned and also develops out of a configuration of geometrical forms that appears in the earlier books. The mandala is a square within a circle, with a symbolic centre that represents the in-dwelling god which is double-natured or hermaphroditic. The square is a symbol for life in the material world, the life trapped in the body and in the house. As has been pointed out earlier, the house is often, by grace of the law of correspondences that operates in White, a symbol of the body, and its occupant thus corresponds to the core of being. The outer circle is the world of Being, which threatens the defensive walls of the four-square house. The end of the spiritual cycle is the transformation of the outer limits of the personality from the square to the circle, a transformation that comes about through resolution of the problem that the fourth element of the quaternity poses. This transformation releases the heart of the mandala which unites with the outer circle, matter having been eliminated.

In *The Living and the Dead*, we see the opposition of the square and the circle in the contrast between the pebbles of Ard's Bay and the square glass box that comes to symbolize everything enclosed and limited in Elyot's adult life. At the moment of rebirth, Elyot rejects the glass box, leaves the square cell of his room and walks off to Victoria's 'fiery hub'. In *The Aunt's Story*, Theodora also leaves the square house and goes down to the circles of spring water. Stan Parker finally abandons the four-square life of his house and finds himself at the centre of a cosmic mandala, of which he is the immanent deity and the outermost circle is the transcendent God. If we stand back from the canvas of *Voss*, we can see a muted expression of the same pattern: the quaternity of visionaries, one of whom is a daemonic odd-man-out, rides into the innermost circle of Hell where Christ appears. The immediate predecessor of the mandalas is, of course, the Chariot, in which the four Living Creatures (the basic component of the Christian mandala) support the Throne and are encircled by the whirlwind. The problem of the quaternity is resolved in this book as the three other Riders cluster around, and are transfigured by their conjunction with, the dying Himmelfarb. The same mandalic pattern appears in many forms in *The Eye of the Storm*, particularly during the climactic moment on Brumby Island where the whirlwind shatters the house and Elizabeth Hunter is allowed a moment of release and tranquillity in the Eye.

This symbolic form, which has been imposing itself unconsciously throughout White's writing, appears as the main organizing principle of *The Solid Mandala*. One of the central problems of this novel is the existence of a flaw at the centre of the fourth mandala. This image appears again in *The Eye of the Storm*: 'She was . . . a flaw at the centre of this jewel of light . . .' (ES p. 424). The flaw of the fourth mandala raises the fundamental problem of the imperfection or evil that is inherent in the 'four-fold', material world.

Of all Arthur's marbles, it is the one with the knot in the centre that he comes to love the best, although he realizes that it is not really his and must, in the end, be discarded (SM p. 228). This marble is Waldo: '"He was born with his innards twisted."' (SM p. 32); 'There was no reason why visitors should have guessed at the flaws in Waldo Brown' (SM p. 75). Arthur's spiritual destiny can be achieved only by accepting full responsibility for Waldo. At the end, however, his selfhood is achieved only when the taint of matter has been purged, and evil has burnt itself out. The quaternity, symbol of matter, is a necessary stage towards the emergence of the One, but that One can only appear when the fourth element is gone, and the structure of the material world which was based on it has crumbled. The irreconcilable cleavage between the quaternity and the One is suggested by a children's song that the brothers hear:

'One a one makes two,'

'One a one a one,' they sang.
'Two a two is never one.' (SM p. 202)

It is only after Waldo has died, and his marble has been lost in the filth and darkness of an alley (SM p. 307), that Arthur can discover his true self. After the loss of Waldo's marble, the first ray of morning light shows him his own mandala on the palm of his hand (SM p. 307) and he knows that he is not destined to die. His apotheosis is achieved through conjunction with Mrs Poulter whom he raises up by giving her an incarnate god to worship after her canvas Christ has fallen, while he himself is completed by being both her Lover and her Son. Nous and Physis complete each other at the centre of the mandala and enter their 'actual sphere of life' (SM p. 317). This parallels the psychic weddings that appear towards the climax of most of the other novels, the conjunctions of Theodora–Holstius, Voss–Laura, Reha–Himmelfarb and Rhoda–Hurtle. After its initial rupture and its necessary, even creative, experience of 'the flaw', the soul is once more unified in preparation for the final Union.

Conclusion:
The Unprofessed Factor

I suppose what I am increasingly intent on trying to do in my books is to give professed unbelievers glimpses of their own unprofessed factor. I believe most people have a religious factor, but are afraid that by admitting it they will forfeit their right to be considered intellectuals. This is particularly common in Australia where the intellectual is a comparatively recent phenomenon. The churches defeat their own aims, I feel, through the banality of their approach, and by rejecting so much that is sordid and shocking which can still be related to religious experience . . . I feel that the moral flaws in myself are more than anything my creative source.

This is what I am trying to do, perhaps more than before in *The Vivisector* which is coming out this year. . . . the novel I am working on at present [*The Eye of the Storm*] . . . seems to have a more specifically religious content and pattern than the others.[19]

These words of Patrick White justify, I feel, the central position that has been assigned in this book to the religious factor in White's writing, and support the eclectic and non-dogmatic approach that has been adopted. This book has committed itself unreservedly to 'the unprofessed factor' as White himself, throughout his writing career, has made this commitment. His work is an attempt to quicken the spiritual faculty in man, a faculty that is so often dismissed, despised or defaced. Beneath the often drab, banal or even ugly surface of Australian society an age-old spiritual drama is being enacted of which the chief protagonist is the human soul. This drama is being played out in the midst of a predominantly secular world where most people are unaware of the issues involved. White has seized these issues, placed them at the centre of his work and bent all his powers of description, dialogue, psychological insight, satire and symbolism to their expression in his art.

Notes

1 Gabriel Marcel, *Being and Having* (translated by A. and C. Black; London, Collins, 1965), pp. 214–15.
2 Cf. the anonymous *The Cloud of Unknowing* (translated into modern English by Clifton Wolters; Harmondsworth, Penguin, 1961).
3 C. G. Jung, *Psychology and Alchemy* (translated by R. F. C. Hull; London, Routledge & Kegan Paul, 1953), p. 60.
4 *Ibid*, p. 289.
5 Martin Buber, *I and Thou* (translated by Ronald Gregor Smith; Edinburgh, T. & T. Clark, 1966), p. 95, p. 96.
6 Simone Weil, *Waiting on God* (translated by Emma Craufurd; London, Routledge & Kegan Paul, 1951), p. 91.
7 *Ibid*, pp. 118–19.
8 *Ibid*, p. 81.
9 *Ibid*, pp. 29–30.
10 Gabriel Marcel, *Being and Having*, pp. 213–14.
11 A. P. Elkin, *The Australian Aborigines* (Sydney, Angus and Robertson, 1938), pp. 240–1.
12 Richard Wilhelm, *The Secret of the Golden Flower* (translated by Cary F. Baynes; foreword and commentary by C. G. Jung; London, Routledge & Kegan Paul, 1962), p. 14.
13 R. D. Laing, *The Divided Self* (Harmondsworth, Pelican Books, 1965), p. 39.
14 *Ibid*, p. 17.
15 Gershom Scholem, *Major Trends in Jewish Mysticism* (New York, Schocken Books, 1961), p. 226, p. 227, p. 235.
16 Cf. Northrop Frye, *Anatomy of Criticism* (Princeton, Princeton University Press, 1957), pp. 131–51.
17 Simone Weil, *Waiting on God*, p. 53.
18 T. S. Eliot, *Collected Poems* (London, Faber and Faber, 1963), p. 20.
19 Extracts from a letter written by Patrick White to Dr Clem Semmler on 10 May 1970. Quoted with the kind permission of Mr White and Dr Semmler.

Index